Praise for 'Faith, Love and Australia'

"*Faith, Love and Australia* is a book that will change minds and hearts.

It is a refreshing and thoughtful reflection by Tony Abbott's prime-ministerial speechwriter on why same-sex marriage embodies the best of conservative ideals.

This book points towards the better Australia that we all seek."

- Alan Jones AO, Broadcaster

"If an institution cannot adapt to community expectations it will not survive. Thankfully these pages contain a comprehensive conservative case for marriage to remain relevant and enduring for all Australians."

- Tim Wilson MP

"This is a book about values in Australian politics, including same-sex marriage. It says that it is not the rejection of conservative values but the 'deepest embrace' of them. David Cameron in Britain advanced, and won, the same proposition with the Tories. It is expressed and explained here in an Australian context which still appears strangely hostile in Robert Menzies "Liberal" Party. Hopefully, not too far into the future it will be lauded as a 'game-changer'."

- Hon Michael Kirby AC CMG, Patron of the Kirby Institute

"This is an important book, which makes a thoughtful and moving case for same-sex marriage, based on the core principles that conservatives hold dear. *Faith, Love and Australia* is a positive book and a must-read for those on my own side of politics."

- Councillor Christine Forster

"This book highlights for Australians what virtually all the Western world has clearly seen: marriage equality is pro-marriage, pro-family, pro-national unity and pro-freedom of choice – all classic conservative values."

– Hon Nick Greiner AC, Former Premier of NSW

FAITH LOVE & AUSTRALIA
The Conservative Case for Same-Sex Marriage

PAUL RITCHIE

Connor Court Publishing

Published in 2016 by Connor Court Publishing Pty Ltd

Copyright © Paul Ritchie 2016

All rights reserved. No part of this book may be reproduced or transmitted in any form or by any means, electronic or mechanical, including photocopying, recording or by any information storage and retrieval system, without prior permission in writing from the publisher.

Connor Court Publishing Pty Ltd
PO Box 7257
Redland Bay QLD 4165

sales@connorcourt.com
www.connorcourt.com
Phone 0497 900 685

ISBN: 9781925501131

Front Cover Design: Simon Moore, Elton Ward Creative

Printed in Australia

For my Mum and Dad.

Fifty years ago they were told they shouldn't marry because they belonged to different churches.

"That we are all, as human souls, of like value cannot be denied. That each of us should have his chance is and must be the great objective of political and social policy."

- Sir Robert Menzies (1945).

Contents

Foreword		11
Preface		17
1	Whereas the People	23
2	The Marriage Advantage	31
3	A Shared Citizenship	51
4	Tradition and Change	77
5	Responsibility and Shame	113
6	Render unto Caesar	133
7	Render unto God	153
8	Answering the Arguments Against Same-Sex Marriage	167
9	The Vote	199
10	The Hope	219
Acknowledgements		227
Bibliography		229
Endnotes		231

Foreword

In public life, there is only one trait more important than the courage of one's own convictions, and that's the courage to change them.

This may seem like an odd statement, especially in an age where every change of position is capable of being characterised as a 'backflip', a 'climb-down', or worse still, 'pandering'; yet it's a thought that runs through every parliamentarian's mind.

In February 2015, I publicly announced my own change of heart on the emotionally charged issue of same-same marriage. For me, the principle of equality before the law would now be my Polaris star in arguing the institution of marriage should be shared with couples of the same sex.

A public change of position is never easy for any parliamentarian. It can be difficult in a personal sense, as well as a political one.

I have been a member of the Liberal Party in Western Australia for almost 30 years, and proudly identify myself as a conservative. For a great bulk of that time I have also been open about being gay, and in 2012 become the first openly gay member of the Federal Parliamentary Liberal Party.

For me, there has never been anything particularly remarkable or contradictory about this, though I have often been bemused by the fact that others seem to feel there is.

Nor at the time did I see anything fundamentally contradictory about being an openly gay man who was opposed to same-sex marriage. That was my honestly held, and deeply considered position for much of my adult life.

I became a Senator in May 2012, and in September of that year the Senate debated the issue of same-sex marriage where I spoke against the motion. My contribution in that debate was a careful articulation of the thinking that had informed my opposition to that point.

In summary, I said not all gays and lesbians supported same-sex marriage; people were confusing the religious institution of marriage with the civil institution; Australians were not yet ready to extend the legal right of marriage to gay and lesbian people; and that the quality of life and gay and lesbian Australians was not limited in any meaningful way because they could not marry. I distrusted the politics and the sloganeering that was 'marriage equality'.

Importantly though, and foreseeing neither future events nor the publication of this book, I observed that change was possible; that "cautious and considered change" was critical if our community were to continue to enjoy the virtues of stability and continuity.

Like equality before the law, stability and continuity are also bedrock principles for conservatives.

Over the time between September 2012 and February 2015, I was conscious that my own attitude to the question of same-sex marriage was undergoing a slow, but steady shift.

An important attribute of being a legislator is the ability to consider issues within a wider framework, and importantly, to reconsider those issues not previously considered more deeply.

As a result, I found that my own thoughts were more rigorously challenging my own biases and assumptions; testing the application of those conservative values which are the bedrock of my worldview.

It's something that occurred slowly, but ultimately I found myself settled in the belief that extending the legal recognition of marriage to same-sex couples complemented, rather than diminished, conservative values.

For me, it was an evolution in thinking, rather than a revolutionary moment or revelation. At their core, conservatives put their trust in evolutionary change, remembering always the famous dictum of Edmund Burke that *"time is required to produce that union of minds which alone can produce all the good we aim at. Our patience will achieve more than our force."*

The decision to go public was not an easy one. I was very conscious there was a risk I may confuse or disappoint many people with my changed stance.

However long ago, I resolved to live my life authentically. In public life as an elected representative, this has translated into an obligation to be honest and open about my thoughts and views on issues, especially on those of great public interest and controversy.

A few days after media reports of my changed position appeared, I received an email from a correspondent heretofore personally unknown to me. In part, it read:

> *"Politics is noble. It is a vocation – and we all bring something to it. Few, however, bring courage. And when courage is combined with grace, it is immensely powerful. The article was a reflection of a life of courage and grace."*

The email was from Paul Ritchie, then speechwriter to Prime Minister Tony Abbott, and the author of the book you now hold in your hands. For me, his words were as timely as they were encouraging.

'Faith, Love and Australia' is not a book for every Australian. It is, however, an important book for conservatives wanting to test their opposition to same sex marriage. It will also be a comfort to those seeking 'permission' to change their view whilst retaining fidelity to conservative principles.

When read with care, it will do two things.

Firstly, it will prick the conscience of genuine conservatives who are interested in extending the application of our most cherished conservative principles to a contemporary reality.

Secondly, the book's eloquence and clear respect for those with opposing views is a powerful demonstration of the good faith in which we conservatives can debate, and even disagree on particular issues, yet still work and feel welcome within the conservative family.

It will also provide a stark delineation between a conservative approach to public discourse, and a reactionary approach. Some people easily confuse the two, but they are quite different.

I have observed after almost 30 years in political life, the last four as a parliamentarian, the risk of being typecast by one's position on issues.

Since announcing my support for same-sex marriage, I have variously been described as a 'moderate', a 'small-l Liberal', and a 'same-sex marriage crusader'. Yet, none of these labels sit comfortably with me.

In hindsight, I should perhaps have expected that Australia's first openly gay Federal Liberal parliamentarian would be regularly asked his views on contemporary controversies involving issues of sexuality.

But I have never seen myself as a 'campaigner' on these issues, and certainly have not sought to be defined solely by my views in this area, nor by my own sexuality.

I hope that in honestly setting out my position, I have helped others – conservatives or not – to understand that for many of our fellow Australians, these matters are deeply felt and deeply personal.

This being the case, we must allow people room to wrestle with their own consciences. In the continuing debate about same-sex marriage, we all have an obligation to treat each other with respect. This obligation applies to people on both sides of the question.

In authoring this book, Paul Ritchie has displayed enormous

courage, and amply demonstrated a commitment to sustaining and extending the principles of conservatism in a modern era. For that, every conservative should give him great applause.

Senator Dean Smith
Perth, Western Australia, June 2016

Preface

THE CONVICTION OF THINGS UNSEEN

If you are driving between Gundagai and Tumut you might see a sign marking the turnoff to the small village of Brungle.

Blink and you miss it.

Brungle is an unremarkable town with a population of just one hundred people. It's not a poor town, but no one is rich either. It no longer has a post office and only nine students attend the local primary school.

The town's most noticeable building is a simple but elegant sandstone church that was built in 1886 and has since been restored to its former glory. As you walk through the town, you wonder how it will survive. But others were saying the same thing about Brungle well over a century ago.

In the late 1800s, the so-called Aborigines Protection Board established the Brungle Mission as the place where the local Wiradjuri people could live.

Don't call it generosity, because it wasn't. The Wiradjuri people had lived in the region for thousands of years. It's just that in more recent times, their presence had been, for all intents and purposes, declared illegal, so the Brungle Mission came into being as a place where the local Aboriginal people could live legally.

The residents of the mission were kin. The children were taught to hunt rabbits, collect firewood, cart water from the local river and respect their elders. The parents, grandparents and 'aunties and uncles' gathered food, undertook work when and where they could, withstood drought and flood, and at night, around the campfire, told the children stories of who they were and the land to which they belonged.

However, it was not an idyllic or romantic place. The mission was little more than a collection of tin shacks lined with old newspapers and hessian bags and a few campfires that provided heat for cooking and warmth.

Despite the connections of kin, the mission was strained by the weight of unquenchable poverty. It was demoralised by the paternalism of its time; by an overly obtrusive government that stripped Aboriginal people of their autonomy, their confidence and at times their children, because government said it knew better than parents.

As one correspondent in the late 1880s wrote in the *Sydney Morning Herald*:

> *Their manner of life is to say the least very forbidding....The Brungle blacks are beggared, and were it not for the kindness of farmers in the district, the women and children would soon be on the verge of starvation, for as soon as the rations are done the men send off their women and children on a begging expedition.*[1]

The people of the Brungle Mission lived hard lives under harsh rules.

While it can be said that many of their white countrymen led lives that weren't much easier, white Australians, unlike their Aboriginal brothers and sisters, were free to live their own lives, cast their own ballots, marry who they saw fit, and raise their children without the interference of strangers.

It was in this most foreboding place that a remarkable moment in Australian history took place.

It occurred in May 1927. Throughout inland New South Wales,

May is that time of year when the warmth of autumn disappears and you wake up to frost on the ground. In May, the mornings are bitter, the clear blue skies of the day mock the lack of warmth of the distant sun and the days shorten as winter approaches.

It was the month when Australia's first Parliament House was to be opened in Canberra. Across the land, over 10,000 of the good and the great were invited to the 'bush capital' to watch the opening by His Royal Highness, the Duke of York – the second son of King George V.

No invitation was sent to Brungle, nor was one expected. In fact, not a single invitation was sent to an Aboriginal in any part of the Commonwealth.

After all, Aboriginals weren't counted in the Census, they weren't counted on the electoral roll, and they weren't allowed to join the armed forces (though some did so during the Great War), so why would anyone expect an Aboriginal to be invited to attend the opening of the Parliament?

However, 80 year-old Jimmy Clements, an elder from the Wiradjuri tribe, decided to go. He knew he had to be in Canberra.

He was old. His country was changing, not necessarily for the better, and it was just possible that Jimmy Clements knew that his time was near. To paraphrase the words of Dylan Thomas he chose to "*not go gentle into that good night*" but to "*Rage, rage against the dying of the light*".[2]

He mattered. His people mattered. This country mattered.

So Clements set out with his companion John Noble, also of the Wiradjuri tribe, and his two dogs on a week-long trek over the mountains.

A 200 kilometre hike is no easy feat, least of all when you are 80 and journeying barefoot, but Jimmy Clements had been walking across the country for most of his life.

Invitation or no invitation, Jimmy Clements was going to attend the most important occasion yet in the history of the Commonwealth of Australia.

Grandstand seating was built to accommodate the thousands who were expected to attend Canberra's greatest event. As the day approached, it was clear the stands would mostly sit empty. The 'bush capital' had little accommodation, car travel was still in its infancy and the journey required at least one night's camping out.

Mostly, the invitations were displayed on mantelpieces and bookshelves as proof of the invitees' importance, but few were willing to camp out in the cold.

In Canberra, all who saw him remembered Clements. His matted white hair and long beard contrasted with the darkness of his skin. The suit he was wearing was thick, almost like canvas and it was covered with the marks of brushed-off dirt, further signs of the long journey he had undertaken. His hat was just as weathered, and one can surmise that after his travels, he smelt of the journey. Amid the finery of the occasion, he was clearly not a man of means, wearing no fur, uniform or overcoat like the other guests photographed on that day.

But he was no vagrant. In his eyes you could see the fierce pride of an ancient people. He may never have read the words of Edmund Burke, but Burke's idea of a compact between the dead, the living and the as yet unborn lived in his bones. It was why he had walked for a week to attend the formalities marking the first monument to this young democracy.

However, that was not appreciated at the time. In the hours before the start of the official ceremony, police officers tried to move Clements on. They saw his presence as an embarrassment. He was an unsightly reminder that Australia was not a white nation.

But when he was asked to move on, the crowd turned on the police. "Leave him alone", they yelled.

"He has more right to be here than anyone", demanded a prominent church minister.

At that moment, the decency of his countrymen was stronger than the officiousness of the authorities – and Clements was allowed to stay put.

When you see the photographs of that day, one thing shines through. It's not the pageantry of the occasion or the finery worn by Australia's foremost citizens, nor is it the dignitaries delivering grand speeches, which in any event were not recorded because the Duke of York lived in fear of his speech impediment (months earlier he had engaged an Australian to help him with that, but that's another story). Rather, it is the photograph of an old Aboriginal man holding an Australian flag.

That's right. Despite everything that had been done to him throughout his life and on that very day, Jimmy Clements was holding an Australian flag.

Jimmy Clements was a patriot.

He had seen our country for what it was, but he chose to believe in what our country could be.

His presence did not shame our country as some imagined it might. It did not shock or offend, indeed the attitude of his countrymen proved otherwise. Instead, his courage, determination, dignity and grace reminded us that we could be and should be more open, more accepting and more decent than we were to him and his kin.

Four months later, just a few miles from Parliament House, Jimmy Clements breathed his last. In keeping with the religious traditions of the day, he was buried in 'unconsecrated ground'. Jimmy Clements could not be buried with the people of faith.

St Paul says that faith *"is the substance of things hoped for and the conviction of things not seen"*. If that is true, and I believe it is, then Jimmy Clements had a deep and living faith in our country.

His faith defied his appalling treatment and circumstances – and it was a faith that did not disappoint.

Eighty-six years after Jimmy Clements witnessed the official opening of the first Parliament House, a smoking ceremony was held to inaugurate the 44th Parliament. At that smoking ceremony held in the Great Hall of 'new' Parliament House stood two proud witnesses, the first Indigenous Member of the House of Representatives and the first female Indigenous Senator.

Australia's 28th Prime Minister Tony Abbott, said at that opening that Jimmy Clements' presence at that original opening in Canberra was as important as that of the future King George VI. As Abbott reminded us, our Australian identity has an Indigenous heritage, a British foundation and a multicultural character – and when we ignore that, it diminishes us all.

Every day during the Abbott Prime Ministership, the picture of Jimmy Clements with his dogs and his flag hung in an office just a few metres from that of the Prime Minister. The image of Jimmy Clements watched over my desk, as it has in almost every political office I have ever worked in.

His story is a reminder that no-one who is an Australian should ever be considered an outsider or denied his full inheritance in his own land; that our country is better when we offer grace rather than take offence; and that we can choose to see our country not for what it is, but for what it can be.

This book is my attempt to keep faith with that legacy. This book is about the Australia that I long for and the Australia that I see.

1

Whereas the People...

> *"Whereas the people of New South Wales, Victoria, South Australia, Queensland, and Tasmania, humbly relying on the blessing of Almighty God, have agreed to unite in one indissoluble Federal Commonwealth..."*
> -Preamble, The Constitution of Australia.

This is not a book that anyone expected Tony Abbott's speechwriter to write. Nor is it a book that I expected to write.

But something happens to every man or woman who becomes a speechwriter to an Australian prime minister. In a way you do not expect, the country that you feel so familiar with, catches you off-guard. The story of Australia comes alive with its joys and triumphs, tragedies and missteps, sacrifices and errors; and all made by the most unlikely people.

It was often late at night, when the Prime Minister and his security detail had called it a day, that there was stillness in the Prime Minister's Office. It was then, when the tumult of the day had passed, that the faint whispers of generations past could be felt and heard.

You could smell the campfires of the Dreamtime as well as the cigarettes and cigars smoked at the constitutional conventions, and hear the yell of goldminers who'd struck it rich and the tap of willow on leather as Bradman hit another four, and you could feel the warm tears of parents holding telegrams in shaking hands, and the sadness of old women remembering the mothers they had been taken from as children.

Those whispers speak of the good and the bad in our national story, of the confusions and disappointments as well as the joys, selflessness and courage that make us who we are.

Australia is not an amorphous mass; it is a tapestry of millions of interconnected lives that reaches back to the dawn of time. We are the only nation in the world that has a continent to itself. It is our land; its institutions and history that have made us who we are.

If there is an idea about Australia that captivated me during my time working for Tony Abbott, it is found at the start of our Constitution: *"the people…have agreed to unite."*

The idea that underpins our country is that we chose to become one people and as a *"common-wealth"* to share one indissoluble future. Our national ideal is not *"the pursuit of happiness,"* or *"liberty, equality, fraternity"*; it is the idea that we will stick by each other and with each other.

It was the genius of our 12th Prime Minister, Sir Robert Menzies that fused together liberal and conservative strands of thinking in our national life. Liberals believe in the individual and in their right to carve out the best path for their own life. A liberal society does not require that we make the same choices or share the same outlook; it only requires that people have access to the same opportunities.

Conservatives understand that our freedoms are derived not from ourselves, but from our social and political institutions. The enduring nature of our freedom, our character and our national unity is found in the institutions that gird our social fabric: families, churches, schools, councils, courts, parliaments and the Crown.

Conservatives are always hesitant to tinker with or alter the social fabric because it is the foundation of our rights and freedoms. This does not mean that institutions should not change. Rather, their change should be evolutionary. Evolutionary change stops our institutions from becoming brittle, sedentary or stagnant, and ensures that they can adapt to the times while retaining their values. The liberal strand also reminds us that institutions are meant to serve the people who created them.

I believe that the move towards same-sex marriage is consistent with both liberal and conservative traditions, and is an evolutionary change that will strengthen the institution of marriage. As the Conservative Prime Minister of the United Kingdom, David Cameron, put it:

> "*Conservatives believe in the ties that bind us; that society is stronger when we make vows to each other and support each other. So I don't support gay marriage despite being a conservative. I support gay marriage because I am a conservative.*"[3]

David Cameron's point is that conservatism is not an ideology, but a way of seeing life. It is not, as some might believe, a philosophy of binding, inflexible rules. Instead, it's a temperament that sees virtue in tradition, duty and the fulfilment of our mutual obligations, and it has a healthy distrust for the bright new idea, for the salesman with the shiny hair and carefree smile, because experience tells us that the best change is incremental.

While the move towards same-sex marriage embodies the values of conservative thinking, it is not conservative orthodoxy. Indeed, it evokes passion among conservatives like few other issues. As the conservative gay author Andrew Sullivan put it:

> "*marriage is alternatively praised and derided as a lynchpin of procreation, love, power, economics, convenience, morality and civil rights. And homosexuality similarly evokes opposing judgments: it is seen as perversion; a source of identity, love and desire; a freely chosen lifestyle, a fabricated personality, a revolution against the status quo. And when these two contested areas are brought together, this matrix of interpretation is multiplied even more, so that, at times, it may seem*

as if no one is even speaking about the same thing."[4]

This book is about unpacking the fears and assumptions that conservatives have about changing a foundational institution. It is about giving conservatives permission to think, argue and question where we stand. After all, if conservatives cannot do this, then how can we say that we are any different from the politically correct who seek to shut down debate and dissent?

For too long, the issue of same-sex marriage has been caught in the logjam of the culture wars and we've all been diminished by it. More than any other debate, it has been characterised by an inability to listen, a casualness in labelling others, a continual questioning of each other's motives and morals, a brutal exploitation of verbal slips, and the use of tactics that are meant to silence and shame.

Although Australians have been talking about same-sex marriage for 15 years, we should not be afraid of reflection and debate. As the NSW Liberal MP, Dominic Perrottet has written, *"True progress demands a truly free exchange of ideas, because the best ideas are forged in the furnace of fierce disagreement – the battle of ideas, where wits are sharpened, arguments blunted, minds expanded, and gradually, truth revealed."*[5] While Dominic Perrottet is a supporter of the status quo when it comes to same-sex marriage, I agree with his sentiments about the value of free debate.

Indeed, the arguments canvassed in this book about conservatism, citizenship, the history of marriage, the interrelationship between church and state, freedom of speech, and identity in a post-Christian age should all be up for debate.

This is not a book that will shout at conservatives and people of faith demanding that they change. If it convinces some people of the arguments for same-sex marriage then, well and good; if it raises questions for others, then let them continue to test the arguments; and if it doesn't convince at all, I will still be grateful that people took the time to consider the case.

In making the conservative case for same-sex marriage, I accept that I bear the burden of proving that change would be a good thing. I also accept that most of those defending the status quo do so with the right motivations.

This book makes the case that allowing same-sex civil marriages is consistent with conservative values. This is a change that's good for the institution of marriage because it means that all Australians will be responsible for upholding it; it's good for gays and lesbians because it gives access to an institution that strengthens relationships; it's good for families because it affirms their gay and lesbian members; it's good for the children of same-sex parents because marriage strengthens the home; and it's good for our country because it expands the freedom of its citizens.

Gays and lesbians do not seek to change marriage, but to join it. It is the embraced truth that marriage is an institution that has virtue and imparts to us a framework that can help us lead happier and more fulfilling lives.

Not all conservatives and people of faith oppose same-sex marriage, just as not all gays and lesbians support it. Our concern should not be who favours or disagrees with same-sex marriage, or what their political persuasion, sexual orientation or religious beliefs might be. Rather, our concern should be to judge the arguments on their merits.

Both the proponents and opponents of same-sex marriage accept that marriage is good for people. It was the 1549 Prayer Book that defined the purpose of marriage as *"mutual society, help and comfort, that the one ought to have of the other, both in prosperity and in adversity."*[16] On this, there is agreement.

We all believe that marriage requires love, commitment and

sacrifice, and its fruits are joy, kindness, laughter and strength in times of difficulty. We know that our deepest needs are not for things, but for each other. Without others to love, we are adrift, neither nourished nor supported as we face the tempest of life.

"For better or worse, richer or poorer, and in sickness and in health, to love and to cherish from this day forward, until death do us part" is a promise that we will not have to face the trials of life alone.

Of course, not everyone aspires to marriage, and no one is arguing that everyone should. We also know enough about the human condition to appreciate that not all marriages will last the distance. We should be accepting about the differing circumstances that we all face because life is easier when there is not judgment on others.

A marriage is more than the promise of two people and their physical union; it is also a promise by society to affirm and support their union. Other than birth and adoption, marriage is the only legal means by which we admit people to our families. Marriage strengthens families, and allowing gay and lesbian members of our families to marry will only make families stronger. This is a conservative ideal.

There is also agreement that religious institutions should be free to administer marriage in accordance with the dictates of their faith. The Constitution and the Marriage Act protect the rights of religious celebrants, and this will not change. The argument for same-sex marriage is about civil marriage, it is not about enforcing changes on religious communities. The only religious groups that would administer same-sex weddings would be those that decide to offer the ceremony as part of their religious tradition.

It is in marriage that we see the intersection of romantic love, family support, mutual reciprocity, law, community, and for many, faith. It is a guidepost for life. Gay, lesbian, transgendered, bisexual and intersex Australians need guideposts and supports as much as anyone else.

The lives of gay, lesbian, bisexual, intersex and transgender Australians are no better and no worse than any others. None of us, straight or gay, are that much different from each other – in the quiet places, where no one sees us but ourselves, we all live out our existence through lives that are as complex, sad, joyous, confused and straight forward as any other. What gives strength and meaning to our world is the knowledge that we are loved.

Marriage can be a powerful affirmation to our lives. A wedding is the day we see our parents' joyful tears and receive their blessing; it is when we hear our best friend's speech with love hidden in the humour; and it is when the love of our life is admitted to our family, and we to theirs. Some people say that marriage does not change people; I don't believe that is true.

Marriage is more than a piece of paper. It is a gentle change in the GPS of our lives that reminds us that we are obligated to someone else. Our focus turns from ourselves to others and we think less about our rights and more about our responsibilities. In so doing, we find further meaning for our lives and we strengthen our families and communities. At its heart, this reflects the conservative hope.

It was Menzies who reminded us that our differences must always hark back to our shared identity as Australians. He argued that it is the sum of who we are as a people that creates a stronger, more virtuous and enduring nation. However, such progress is more difficult to achieve when all citizens do not share the same opportunities.

Marriage is a civil institution as well as a religious one. Although we are a people informed by faith, we are not a people ruled by faith or who persecute faith. We live in a world where tolerance is under threat. In some places, gay men are thrown off buildings and hacked and stoned to death, and Christians are treated similarly. More than ever, Western democracies must stand for the rights of all citizens to live out their lives, free of coercion and persecution. The answer to intolerance is always a greater acceptance of difference.

Allowing same-sex couples to marry is not just a matter of law. It's also a matter of heart and soul. The institution of marriage affirms us as people, gives standing to our most significant relationship and changes our families for the better. It is an institution that points to a better life and helps us to answer the deepest question: can I selflessly love another and find meaning and purpose in that love? This too is a conservative ideal.

This book will put the case that same-sex marriage affirms individuals, strengthens families and is a reflection of our shared citizenship. In every sense, it is a reflection of conservative values.

I have chosen in this book not to use the term 'LGBTI' because I can't reduce people to 'a letter of the alphabet'. We are all so much more than that. For simplicity, I will often use the term 'gays and lesbians', which can be considered as shorthand for all sexualities seeking the opportunity to marry.

I have also chosen not to use the popular political frame 'marriage equality', because same-sex marriage is about more than equality. It is not about ticking a box on legal rights, it is about something more important: it is about believing that gay, lesbian, bisexual, transgender and intersex Australians can have lives as noble, meaningful and selfless as those of anyone else.

This is easy to believe because it reflects the daily truth of our Australian lives – where we see the service and devotion of gay, lesbian, bisexual, transgender and intersex Australians in our communities, in our workplaces and in our families.

It is about no longer seeing a separate *'them'*, but about realising that *'they'* are part of *'us'*.

Then, once again, we will be able to say...*the people agreed to unite.*

2

THE MARRIAGE ADVANTAGE

If marriage was *'just a piece of paper'*, that did not change our lives, our relationships and the trajectory of our families, then the debate on same-sex marriage would be nothing more than another skirmish in the culture wars. But marriage is much, much more than a piece of paper.

Both sides in this debate have something in common: they share a deep respect for the institution that has shaped our civilisation, our country and our families. It goes to the heart of who we are as humans. As Kevin Andrews wrote:

> *"To be loved and accepted, and to feel part of something greater than ourselves are amongst the deepest yearnings of the human heart."*

In putting the case for marriage, I accept that marriage is not for everyone. One in three Australian marriages is not lifelong, although not all marriages that end need be called failures. A friend of mine remarked, after seeing an obituary of his father with the words 'failed marriage' in it, "I *don't know why it used the word 'failed'. Mum and Dad were together for thirty years. They raised three children, including one with a disability, and we all get on exceptionally well. Their marriage might have ended but there is still a loving family in place".*

In putting the case for marriage, I do not judge those who aren't married or those who were once married but are no longer. The vicissitudes of life touch us all. What happens within a marriage is so often a mystery, even to those within it.

At the time of writing, I have been married for 18 years. Like all couples, Sarah and I have made our sacrifices, accommodations and compromises, and we have met our share of disappointments as well as triumphs. What matters in our forties seems so far away from what we thought mattered in our twenties. Still, when I walk through the door at night, I feel at home; our girls know they are loved by their mum and dad, and there is a familiarity with each other that has its comforts and strength. I walk life's journey with someone who is a familiar and kind face and in the dark moments, that makes all the difference.

Marriage is a hope, and at times, a struggle. In that regard, it mirrors life itself.

A happy marriage is of great benefit to the husband and the wife, to the couple as an entity, to their children and to society. People who are married live longer, are wealthier, are happier and are strengthened by each other as they are carried by the currents of life. Some researchers have called the quantum of benefits that come from marriage the 'marriage advantage'.

The reason why the case for same-sex marriage is compelling is because the case for marriage is compelling. The 'marriage advantage' permeates our health, our relationships, our finances, and our wellbeing. Understanding the 'marriage advantage' is essential to understanding why same-sex marriage matters.

The marriage advantage: physical health

The health benefits of marriage have been proven in hundreds of studies.[7]

Married people live longer than single people.[8]

They drink less and take fewer illicit drugs.[9]

They smoke less and find it easier to give up smoking.[10]

They are safer on the roads.[11]

They eat more healthy food.[12]

They cope better, and they have lower rates of cardiovascular disease and hypertension.[13]

For most of the major causes of death, marriage protects you.

Being married is not an incantation that means a married man or woman does not need to do regular exercise, or take care of himself or herself. These are averages, and other factors such as genetics and lifestyle will inevitably play a part. Given that these are averages, some will experience more and others less of a beneficial benefit, and for every measure there will be some who defy the odds completely. My grandmother lived until she was 90, and she smoked every day of her adult life. We know that smoking kills, but it didn't kill her. However, one person's story does not disprove a fact. All of us, in our own ways, will out-perform or under-perform the averages, but that does not alter the fact that marriage is good for your health.

Researchers surmise that this is the result of three factors. First, when there is someone else around, they tend to remind us to eat better, sleep more, take care of ourselves or visit a doctor, even if we don't think we need to. There is someone to care for us – to watch out for us. Second, we tend to take better care of ourselves if we feel that our lives matter to others. Third, in ways most of us do not understand, there is a deep interrelationship between our physical health and our emotional wellbeing. Marriage helps us to feel better about ourselves and our lives, and provides comfort and succour when we need it.

The studies also find that the health benefits are greater for men than for women. This could reflect the fact that women, no matter what the circumstances, can organise themselves into communities of support, or that men are more likely to undertake activities that are unhealthy when they are alone. It could also be that the care of a woman touches a man.

Whatever the reason, all the evidence is conclusive – having someone who cares for you – and who at times, is caring for you – is good for your health.

The marriage advantage: mental health

A happy marriage is also good for your emotional health.

Marriage is a vital source of companionship, intimacy and social support.

Research demonstrates that, on average, married people are emotionally happier than single people.

The Australian Institute of Family Studies, a Federal Government agency charged with studying issues and trends in family life, agrees that a happy marriage is good for your emotional health.[14]

It points to a body of research demonstrating better outcomes in relation to happiness, depression, life satisfaction, psychological wellbeing and mortality from suicide. These outcomes are not unique to Australia, and can also be seen in research findings from New Zealand, the United States, Europe and Asia.

According to the Melbourne Institute's longitudinal study "The Household, Income and Labour Dynamics in Australia (HILDA) Survey", people who are living alone feel more isolated than those living with others. The HILDA study found that:

- People who live with others have a greater sense of *"high social support"* than those who live alone (71 per cent vs 63

per cent);
- People who live alone are more likely to feel lonely than those who don't (26 per cent vs 16 per cent); and
- People who live alone are more likely to get bored than those who live with others (39 per cent vs 31 per cent).

Having someone to talk to, someone who watches out for you, and provides company at the end of a long day, helps make all the difference as we face the challenges of life.

As well, marriage broadens the range of people in our world and expands the social networks in our lives. About one in every four people, myself included, are believed to be introverts. Mostly, introverts draw strength from within, but sometimes there is no strength to be found. It is during these times that marriage (as well as a few good friends) can bring emotional sustenance to one's inner world.

Marriage also brings its own security. It reduces emotional ambiguity with the two partners entering into the relationship with the belief that it will be permanent.

A 20-year study by German researchers found increased satisfaction throughout marriage.[15] An 18-year longitudinal study in the Netherlands produced similar findings.[16] In the United States, the National Survey of Families and Households found an increase in happiness and a decline in the incidence of depression.[17]

Some have argued that it is possible that marriage 'pre-selects' people, in that it attracts people who yearn for the stability and longevity of marriage. Even if that is true, this does not negate the fact that for most people marriage is good for their mental health.

The marriage advantage: financial security

While we will see in Chapter 4 how the institution of marriage has evolved over time, one thing that has not changed is the link between marriage and financial security.

True, the marriage contract is no longer negotiated in a notary's office, nor are there dowries or payments between families, but marriage is still an important means by which individuals secure their financial future.

The partners in a marriage achieve economies of scale — and it's more than just buying one toaster instead of two. It can mean pooling resources to pay off debt quicker and obtaining a joint loan for their first property. Having two incomes allow us to spread the risk as we navigate the ebbs and flows in our working lives.

Across most measures — income, wealth, superannuation savings and reliance on one's self rather than on government, married people and couples in long-term relationships outperform single people.

According to the Australian Bureau of Statistics (ABS), 48 per cent of adult Australians are married, 34 per cent have never been married, 11 per cent are separated or divorced and 6 per cent are widowed.

When we splice ABS household data another way, we find that 71 per cent of households are family households (married and de facto couples with or without children), 24 per cent of households are lone person households and 5 per cent of households are mixed-family households.

On most economic measures, couples are more secure than single people. We can confirm this by looking at three key measures of economic security: housing, income and wealth.

Housing

We see stronger outcomes for couples in terms of household living arrangements.

Australians recognise that purchasing and paying off the family home is a vital way to secure their economic future.

In households paying off mortgages, 66 per cent are being paid off by couples and 12 per cent are being paid off by single people.[18]

In households in which the property has been paid off, 49 per cent are owned by couples and 32 per cent are owned by single people. On the surface, this appears to be a better outcome for single people (given that only 24 per cent of households are single person households), until you notice that the average age in these households is 66. The figure of 32 per cent for single-person households is inflated by widows and widowers.

In relation to rented accommodation, we see statistics that better reflect the general population, with couples and families accounting for 44 per cent of rental households and singles accounting for 25 per cent.

Strikingly, 50 per cent of all public housing tenants are single people, whereas only 12 per cent are couples.[19]

Income

Most couples pool their income – '*yours*' and '*mine*' becomes '*ours*'. That is not to say every couple does the same thing. My parents have kept separate bank accounts for 50 years and regularly 'borrow' from each other. I roll my eyes and wonder what will happen if they ever call each other on the money they have borrowed. Whereas Sarah and I have one account, and keep a close eye on the balance as we get close to pay day.

While married couples have the benefit of pooling income, it is a necessity when raising children. According to the ABS, the average couple with dependent children has a median weekly income of $2,313 and an equivalised disposable household income of $868.[20]

By comparison, couples without children have a median income of $1,421 per week and an equivalised disposable household income of $890 per adult. These results are not surprising as this group is a younger group (on average) than couples with children and less advanced in their careers. As they do not have the expense of children, their disposable incomes are slightly higher than those of couples with dependent children.

However, when we look at the incomes for single-person households we see significantly different numbers. In no age group is the equivalised disposable household income for singles higher than that for couples without dependent children. Turning to couples with dependent children, we again see that couples outperform singles with one exception – when the couple has a dependent child aged 5 or less. This is understandable given that often one parent stays at home (or reduces their work hours) to look after the child.

	Median Gross Income	
	Single	Couple
With Children	• Average: $1,053	• Children age <5: $2,160 • Children age 5-14: $2,373 • Children age >15: $2,532
Without Children	• Age <35: $1,058 • Age 35-54: $1,010 • Age 55-64: $679 • Age >65: $480	• Age < 35: $2,252 • Age 35-54: $2,159 • Age 55-64: $1,626 • Age >65: $844

	Equivalised disposable income	
	Single	Couple
With Children	• Average: $563	• Children age <5: $835 • Children age 5-14: $861 • Children age >15: $933
Without Children	• Age <35: $899 • Age 35-54: $864 • Age 55-64: $649 • Age >65: $479	• Age < 35: $1,241 • Age 35-54: $1,192 • Age 55-64: $953 • Age >65: $560

Australian Bureau of Statistics. Cat No. 6523.0 Household Income and Wealth, Australia, 2013-14 Table 11.1

Wealth

It is not surprising that these differences in income between couples and singles eventually manifest themselves in differences in the financial worth of households.

Couples are a more attractive proposition for banks to lend to for housing and investments. They support each other in the running of small businesses, and they can temper each other, when one partner wants to buy a new car or go on an extravagant holiday.

As expected, average household wealth hits its peak as people end their working lives (the 55 - 64 age group). For couples in this demographic, average household wealth is just over $1.6 million. For the single person it is $667,000. If we make the comparison on an individual basis, a married or de facto partner in this age group has a net worth of $800,000, which is more than 20 per cent greater than that of their single counterpart.

The only age group where, on an individualised basis, singles outperform couples are the under 35s and the over 65s. The over 65s is understandable given that it includes widows and widowers who have inherited their late spouse's assets.

	Household Net Worth	
	Single	Couple
With Children	• Average: $371,000	• Children age <5: $597,300 • Children age 5-14: $942,800 • Children age >15: $1,304,600
Without Children	• Age <35: $156,400 • Age 35-54: $398,200 • Age 55-64: $667,800 • Age >65: $696,000	• Age < 35: $270,000 • Age 35-54: $814,000 • Age 55-64: $1,607,000 • Age >65: $1,383,100

Australian Bureau of Statistics: Cat No. 6523.0 Household Income and Wealth, Australia, 2013-14. Table 11.2

Superannuation

One area that contributes to this discrepancy in wealth is superannuation. By anecdote and experience, couples prepare for their retirement earlier than single people.

A typical couple in the 54 – 65 age group has $488,000 in their combined superannuation account. This compares with $143,100 for a typical single person in the same age group. Put another way, the average amount in the superannuation account of a husband or wife in this age group is $244,000 which is 70 per cent more than that of their single counterparts.

Maybe the experience of watching children grow up so fast, makes you realise that time moves quicker than you think. Or it could be that the mindset of providing for your family makes you actively consider preparing for your own retirement. No matter the cause, the evidence indicates that couples prepare for their retirement better than their single counterparts.

	Superannuation	
	Single	Couple
With Children	• Average: $57,900	• Children age <5: $100,800 • Children age 5-14: $166,800 • Children age >15: $316,900
Without Children	• Age <35: $23,400 • Age 35-54: $80,400 • Age 55-64: $143,100 • Age >65: $78,900	• Age < 35: $52,400 • Age 35-54: $171,500 • Age 55-64: $488,100 • Age >65: $256,700

Australian Bureau of Statistics: Cat No. 6523.0 Household Income and Wealth, Australia, 2013-14. Table 11.2

The marriage advantage: it's good for families

A world without marriage is a world full of sex, but not full of love. It is a world where we fear abandonment, sickness or old age, a world of short-term relationships, of the sugar hit of romantic love – but not of the companionship of a shared life.

Marriage civilises us, which is why marriage and the resulting family is the cornerstone of civilisation.

In this proposition, we see the proponents and opponents of same-sex marriage agree: stable, happy and loving marriages are vital for the health of our society

As the former head of the Australian Christian Lobby, Jim Wallace, says: "*A large number of the current problems encountered by society are caused by family breakdown. As a society we need to be doing all we can to promote stable marriages and family life, not changing what marriage means.*"[21]

I agree with his premise. Stable family life is vital. Where we differ is in the conclusion. Pulling the drawbridge up and saying "no more" is not the way we strengthen families; rather, it is through welcoming and accepting all who want to share in family life.

Other than birth and adoption, marriage is the only way we admit people into families. Girlfriends, boyfriends and live-in partners may enjoy the company of their partner's family and they may receive care, kindness and love from that family, but they are not kin.

Marriage is the way we legally make our partners part of our family. It removes any relational ambiguity. No longer is a partner a guest at a family gathering; rather, he or she is a member. No longer are they an outsider but a contributor to the loving force of a family.

For conservatives, family and its centrality are in our bones. The shared stories of times past, the joy in celebrating birthdays, christenings and weddings, and the wistful recollections at funerals are reminders that our foundational identity as people is found in our family life.

Before we are anything in this world, we are first a son or daughter, a grandson or granddaughter, a sister or brother, a nephew or niece or a cousin to many. It is to our family that we first belong.

Our families grow and change as new members are born or admitted into them. Sons can marry their girlfriends, daughters can marry their boyfriends and bring them home and make them kin. But our sons and daughters who are gay or lesbian cannot. They can bring their partners to dinner, they can laugh and cry with us, but according to the law, the guests at the dinner table will never be family; they will always be just visitors.

Domestic life is a good thing for all of us. In not allowing family members to marry the person they love, we are asking them to be part of domestic life without a blessing, without society's affirmation and without the right of passage that turns a stranger into family.

For most gay couples, there won't be children for them or grandchildren for their parents, but there will be birthdays, Christmases, meals, baby sitting of nieces and nephews, job losses and promotions, as well as visits to nursing homes and funerals.

Marriage and its capacity to make our partners 'kin' is a foundation by which we can fortify ourselves as we travel through the tempest of life.

Marriage is an affirmation of all that we can be. To share a life with another requires us to think of more than ourselves. It is the roadmap by which the full immersion in the love of family gives us confidence to tackle life.

Children

Stable and strong families are vital in giving children the best start in life.

Marriage provides children with stability. It provides legal protection, emotional stability and social legitimacy, and sends a message to children that mum and dad will always be there for them.

Providing children with love and an abiding sense of security is the primary responsibility of every parent. As John Stuart Mill put it, "*a human life can be a blessing or a curse – unless we give that life an ordinary chance of a good existence, it is a crime against that being.*"[22]

The marvel of children is that, mostly, they make their parents' relationship stronger. They turn a couple into a family. Children are the pillars of a family. This doesn't mean that a couple without children is any less loving or meaningful, but children change a couple for the better. The 'us' becomes bigger, and the shared mission of raising children brings its own meaning and joy.

Research also points to a slightly lower divorce rate for couples with children. The shared welfare of the children, and the realisation that home means 'spouse and children' become reasons to stay together when the storms of life hit.

And the storms of life do hit – with one in three marriages not going the distance, and almost one in two marriages that end in divorce involving children.[23]

Marriage, with its legal, familial and social supports, strengthens couples. It is fundamental to the wellbeing of children, but it is also so much more. In the words of Jonathan Rauch, *"It is also about happiness, security, safety, prosperity, good health, sound mind, altruism, personal growth, sex, – and – did I almost forget, love."*[24]

Our homes and relationships are more stable because of the institution of marriage. This is another reason why marriage is good for people.

The marriage advantage: marriage is good for society

The foundation of society is the family. Without a stable foundation, our society pays a heavy price.

As Sir Robert Menzies said more than half a century ago:

> "I do not believe that the real life of this nation is to be found in either great luxury hotels and the petty gossip of so called fashionable suburbs, or in the officialdom of organised masses. It is to be found in the home of people who are nameless and unadvertised, and who, whatever their individual religious conviction or dogma, see in their children their greatest contribution to the immortality of their race. The home is the foundation of sanity and sobriety; it is the indispensable condition of continuity; its health determines the health of society as a whole."[25]

Menzies' argument is not new. Three centuries before Christ, Aristotle argued that if children did not love their parents and family, they would love no one but themselves. If we are not for our family, we cannot be for our community, and that means the only thing we stand for is ourselves.

Families are the bridge between the individual and society. As we walk through city streets, we often see men and women caught in addiction, struggling to make it through another day. Before anyone is ever lost to society, they are first lost to family. It is family that is the safety net that helps us through the worst of life. It is why we should be strengthening our families and supporting those who make lifelong commitments to do so.

Self-reliance

Some have argued that government has no place in the regulation of civil marriage, that it is another area of state intrusion and red tape.

The irony is that this is one area that, outside of the marriage licence, the government actually does not regulate. It does not prescribe when family meals are held, what the sleeping arrangements are in a household or who makes dinner or takes out the garbage. In this arena, government knows its limits, and couples are left to make the best arrangements to suit themselves. Rightly, government only intervenes if the security or safety of a spouse or child is threatened.

However, government does have an interest in marriage. It should desire that marriage thrives, because marriage makes the job of government easier. It is the family that is the first safety net. It is the spouse who says you need a doctor to check that cough, or that your drinking is spiralling out of control, or that the superannuation accounts need topping up, or who takes on an extra load with the children when you have other commitments.

For most of my married life I have been the principal breadwinner and Sarah has got the kids off to school and made my life easier. As I write this book, I am between jobs and Sarah is bringing in an income. It's my turn to take the kids to school and drop them off and pick them up at soccer and water polo. Our safety net is each other.

Before we turn to the state for help, married couples turn to each other. In families we have the support structure that helps us cope when adversity hits. A child, a teenager, a man or a woman can rise again if they know they have the support of their family.

The family is society's best safety net. Government has a legitimate interest in encouraging lifelong committed relationships because it strengthens the social fabric and reduces the demands on government. It's another reason why marriage reflects a conservative ideal and why it should be extended to gay and lesbian Australians.

Welfare

For married couples, the family is the safety net. We see this reflected in data about welfare and couples. Couples are less likely to need welfare than single people.

While I subscribe to the Menzian view that it's always better to be a contributor than to be a receiver, I also recognise that a strong and fair safety net is a reflection of a decent and just society.

Right across the demographic data presented in this chapter, there is one group that stands out in terms of its under-performance in relation to income, wealth, superannuation and having a heavy reliance on welfare, and that group is single parents with dependent children. It is a tough journey, and I wonder how they do it. I also question whether we are doing enough to help single parents onto a path of self-sufficiency and self-security. Welfare is expensive, and the needs are growing, particularly as we seek to fund Australians with limited retirement savings, but still, helping children to get a decent start in life will pay long-term dividends for our country.

As can be seen from the table, single people across all demographics have a greater reliance on government for welfare payments than couples. For all the talk of 'middle-class welfare' and overly generous family support, the data indicates that it is mostly single people who draw on the safety net of government. This is another reason why government has an interest in encouraging and supporting long-term relationships.

Proportion of household income that is based on government welfare payments

	20% to less than 50%	50% to less than 90%	90% and over
Couple only under 35	1.8%	1.0%	1.2%
Lone person under 35	1.9%	3.6%	7.1%
Couple with dependent children	11.5%	3.7%	3.6%
Couple with non-dependent children	13.6%	5.3%	5.6%
Single parent with dependent children	21.0%	21.0%	21.9%

Couple only (all couples without dependents)	6.2%	11%	15.2%
Lone person (all singles)	4.1%	11.1%	32.4%
Couple over 65	11.7%	26.5%	33.9%
Lone person 65 and over	7.9%	21.9%	54.1%

(Australian Bureau of Statistics. 6523.0 Household Income and Income Distribution 2011-2012)

Crime

Marriage is both an institution and a practice. In the words of American academic James Q. Wilson, *"As an institution, it deserves unqualified support; as a practice, we recognise that married people are as imperfect as anyone else."*[26]

This is true, but the power of marriage to domesticate men is well known – and it's not just marriage that does it, it's also the prospect of marriage. Marriage as well as children domesticates men; it reminds them that other people are depending on them. It changes the balance as we make decisions that involve risk.

Some might say this is a female influence and I'm receptive to that thought, but it could also be that a day-by-day, week-by-week, month-by-month and year-by-year devotion to another person domesticates us.

A 53 year longitudinal study that followed the lives of 500 high-risk males (from age 17 to 70) found that marriage inhibits the propensity for men, particularly younger men, to commit crime.

Marriage creates the daily routines and interlocking defences of obligation, mutual support and restraint that discourage criminal propensities within some men. The study also found that men who offend are less likely to re-offend because marriage offers post-prison life structure and support.

In the words of the study report:

> *"Marriage has the potential to 'knife-off' the past from the present in the lives of disadvantaged men and lead to one or more of the following: opportunities for investment in new relationships that offer social support, growth, and new social networks; structured routines that centre more on family life and less on unstructured time with peers; forms of direct and indirect supervision and monitoring of behaviour; or situations that provide an opportunity for identity transformation and that allow for the emergence of a new self."*[27]

As another social researcher put it, it is the *"movement from a hell raiser to a family man."*

Some could argue that this longitudinal study demonstrates the beneficial effect of women on men's lives, and I'm happy to accept that argument. But we should also recognise that all of us benefit from love and attachment, commitment and loyalty, and from the testing that comes from sharing your life with others.

It is not only men who benefit from marriage; our wider society also benefits as marriage helps men to make better choices in their lives.

The marriage advantage: the nation

Across all measures, marriage offers significant benefits to individuals, to couples, to families, to communities and to our country.

Our lives are better because other people are married. Our lives are stronger, our families are happier, and our communities are closer, because millions of our fellow citizens have made vows to love, honour and cherish another person. Because others have made the social fabric stronger, the benefits flow through to all of us. This is the marriage advantage for our civilisation.

Marriage is good, although it is not necessarily for everyone. For the spontaneous and the independent, marriage might not suit their yearnings, but for most of us it creates a foundation for our adult life. The interdependence of marriage provides us with certainty and security, as well as companionship, mutual support and shared lives.

Those who are married understand that it is not a right or a privilege, but a responsibility to care for another, and to invite them to care for you.

Mostly, it is a virtuous cycle, for marriage makes people happier and happier people have better marriages. It still is life's best hope.

If marriage represents a hope, or an invitation to take responsibility, why would we seek to deny others the opportunity to experience it? What benefit is there to us and to our country in denying the benefits of marriage to others?

Gays and lesbians do not seek to change marriage, nor to challenge it or take it by force. Instead, gays and lesbians simply seek the opportunity to marry, to partake in its fruit and to share in its inheritance.

3

A Shared Citizenship

If there is a time in our history that defines innocence, courage, patriotism, tragedy and folly, it is the Great War.

From a population of just under 5 million people, 417,000 men enlisted, 152,000 were wounded and 61,000 made the ultimate sacrifice. Untold more returned home a shell of their former selves.

The war upended almost every Australian family. One in every two Australian men under the age of 42 enlisted.

One of those men was Norman Gibbins, a 34 year-old bachelor from Sydney. Gibbins was one of the first to enlist in the Australian Infantry Force when war was declared in July 1914 and he was given the service number of 86.[28]

When he enlisted, Norman Gibbins fudged the answer to one question on his enlistment form. It asked *"Who is your next of kin?"* and he wrote *"None."* Of all his answers on that enlistment form, it was the only one to which he added a definitive full stop.

The truth is that Norman Gibbins had a family. He had a mother, a father, two sisters and a brother, but he had not spoken to his mother, his father or his brother or a sister for 10 years. He was, however, very close to his sister Violet, so much so that he carried with him a book of pressed Australian flowers that she had given him before he left our shores.

Norman Gibbins went ashore at Gallipoli on that first ANZAC Day in 1915, and was hit in the shoulder and wounded during the

Gallipoli campaign. By 1916, he had been promoted to the rank of Captain and was fighting on the Western Front.

In typical Australian fashion, Gibbins' comrades shortened his name to 'Gibb', and he was universally admired by his peers. Gibb, in the words of Australia's official war historian Charles Bean, was *"Six foot four in his boots, a gaunt, brave, humorous, cool headed Australian, bank manager in civilian life, older than most company officers, but an athlete, promoted from the ranks of ANZAC."*[29]

There was a gentleness about Gibb that was apparent to all, but this didn't mean that he was weak or battle shy. As a soldier, he was smart and calculating, gave as good as he got, and didn't take unnecessary risks with his men.

Gibb had that rare mix of wisdom, compassion, bravery and selflessness that reflected a life that had been tested by adversity. In Bean's words, Gibb's men *"almost worshipped him"*. Other than his beloved sister, to whom he wrote regularly, these comrades had become his family. He was devoted to them and repeatedly risked all for them.

On one occasion, he heard whimpering in 'no man's land' and thinking it was one of his men, he and another soldier sought out the source of the noise only to find a bloodied German soldier. Instead of leaving him to die, Gibb and the other soldier took him prisoner and carried him back to the Australian line to get the medical help that he so desperately needed.

It was in July 1916 during the Battle of Fromelles that Gibb faced his greatest test. His battalion, the 55th, could not hold the ground that they had captured earlier. They were caught up in a maelstrom of bombs and shrapnel, and in danger of being cut off. Annihilation awaited them. The order was given to retreat, and the Australians had to make a dash for it.

But you can't just run with your backs to the enemy. Someone must hold the rear guard, and that man was Norman Gibbins. As his men made their retreat, Gibb put himself between the Germans and his men.

He was the last to vacate the trench, not leaving until he was sure that no man had been left behind. When he was certain they had got away, he started to make his own way along the trench towards the Australian line, but it was impassable. The trench was blocked with the bodies of dead and wounded Australian soldiers.

Seeing the congestion, Gibb left the trench so that he could clamber over the parapet. As he raised himself above the parapet and took one last look behind him, Captain Norman Gibbins, Service Number 86, was struck in the head by a bullet and died instantly. Another Australian soldier lost to the futility of war.

But Norman Gibbins' life had not been futile, for he lives on in the story of our nation. As Charles Bean wrote:

> *"You will not find him where he ought to be – in the hall of V.C's: yet, like many who best earned that distinction, I do not think he would have sought it, resting content with a reward infinitely more precious – the adoring trust, and gratitude of his mates, and the consciousness that, in an hour of need, he had served Australia well."*[30]

But the story of Captain Norman Gibbins does not end with his death. In the years that followed, there was an acrimonious family dispute. His sister Violet, the beneficiary of his will and armed with letters from her late brother, asked for his medals, but so did his estranged mother.

Medals cannot be willed, as they are the gift of the government, and precedent demands that they be given to the next of kin, but Norman Gibbins had been clear, that if he were awarded any medals, they should go to his sister. In his sister's words, his parents were *"a disappointment"* to him.

It was a dispute that would have tested the wisdom of Solomon, and it lasted for four years until eventually, in keeping with Solomon's most famous decision, the medals were split between the mother and the sister.

Along the way, Norman's brother tried to explain to the Australian Army why there had been such an acrimonious split in his family. In a code that the army officers would understand, he wrote that his bachelor brother lived a life that was explainable though deplorable.

The inference was unmistakable. Norman Gibbins had been a homosexual.

We cannot verify the brother's inference. It could be true or it could have been a final salvo from a terrible family schism. Either way, it doesn't matter, because we know that a person's sexuality is not their character. The history books testify to Norman Gibbins' character, and it shines through the ages. But we know from the sweep of human history and our lived experience that beneath the shores and soil of Gallipoli, Lone Pine, the Sinai, Pozieres, Villers-Bretonneux and elsewhere lie the remains of 60,000 Australian men who made the ultimate sacrifice during the Great War, of whom perhaps 1,800 to 2,100 were gay.

Not that these soldiers, and thousands of other soldiers who returned to Australia, would have called themselves gay, or possibly understood the silent currents that ran within them, but they are part of the soul of our country and their sacrifice attests to lives of courage, service and dedication.

A century on, we know of their sacrifice, but we will never know what was in their hearts, for their yearnings and desires were kept hidden because they had been criminalised. To the outside world, these men were heroes, but in their inner worlds, they wrestled with their innate criminality. They could win VCs, be immortalised forever as our Anzacs, but the shame of admitting that they were gay, or being called that derogative term 'a poof', was too great to allow them to do anything other than remain silent.

Today, there are thousands of lesbian, gay, bisexual, transgender and intersex members of the Australian Defence Force (ADF). These men and women live out a citizenship that all Australians respect. Like the men of Norman Gibbins' era, they have sworn an oath to defend our country and protect it from harm. I like to think that Norman Gibbins would be proud of them and proud of the country we have become.

Although these men and women of the ADF offer to lay down their lives for us, our parliament still struggles to trust them with the full expression of citizenship: to live as they choose, to love as they want and to have their relationships accepted as being just as valid as those of anyone else.

Our citizenship is a responsibility. If we ask our gay and lesbian citizens to risk their lives for our country, or to sit on our courts and in our parliaments, and to pay their taxes so that other Australians can have a better life, then surely it is also time to entrust them with the only privilege denied to them – the privilege of getting married, if they so choose.

Our shared citizenship

In Tony Abbott's speech at Lone Pine on the one hundredth anniversary of the Gallipoli landing, the Prime Minister spoke of our national identity: *"Our nation is not just a place on a map, or a mass of people who happen to live somewhere. Our nation is shaped by our collective memory; by the compact, between the dead, the living and the yet-to-be-born."*[31]

Tony Abbott's point is that being an Australian is a shared experience. You cannot be an Australian alone, because being an

Australian means being connected to 24 million other people, as well as all those who have gone before us and who will follow us.

The term 'Australian' has no gender; it has no pre-conditions other than citizenship and it speaks of equality for all who call themselves an 'Aussie'. To be an Australian presupposes a shared belonging to the land, to the people and to its future. It also presupposes that we share similar values. After all, what does it mean to be called an Australian if our citizens do not have any values or hopes in common?

Underpinning it all is the implicit belief that all citizens have the same legal rights and obligations.

Our common citizenship and the story it represents is an essential part of our social fabric. It is a reflection of our rights, our responsibilities and the relationship that exists between government and the governed. When we diminish some citizens, we diminish the citizenship of all.

The question of citizenship and belonging is not a new one. In the early 1700s, Adam Smith argued that the functioning of an economy and a society requires individuals to do things for other people. He argued that an individual understands the shared benefit of being bound to others.

In 1790, Edmund Burke argued that it was our affections for each other in our communities and localities that held us together. He wrote that:

> "*to be attached to the subdivision, to love the little platoon we belong to in society, is the first principle (the germ as it were) of public affections. It is the first link in the series by which we proceed toward a love to our country and to mankind.*"[82]

Being an Australian is not about being part of an amorphous, homogeneous mass, rather it is the sum of many parts that when brought together create something of heart and soul, that is beyond our own self-interest.

It was Menzies who pointed out that our communities and identities are not meant to fray our social fabric. Instead, they should strengthen our common and shared identity as Australians. It is in our shared citizenship that we should find the freedom to be ourselves. As he said:

> *"More and more everybody will come to realise that this is a country in which every community may form part of a greater community and that a tolerant one.*
>
> *There are a lot of people you will encounter who think that we all ought to be the same, that there ought to be a species of drab uniformity, that they all ought to be like me so to speak, that they all ought to be like you, so to speak.*
>
> *This passion for uniformity is not to be encouraged. What we need in Australia is that every person coming from some particular race or faith who comes into the Australian community should retain his quality in that sense but should add it to the qualities of all the other people in the community so that finally we get a powerful structure, a self-respecting structure, a community of high ideals and of clear faith and of generosity and of understanding. Therefore, be yourselves..."*[83]

In an age where our differences in identity seem to be testing our social fabric, where people are identifying more in terms of their ethnic, religious, political and sexual identities than their national citizenship, Menzies' argument is that the various parts of who we are must strengthen the core that we share. We can and must find commonality in our differences, because that is the source of our national cohesion.

That commonality can only be found when we see each other's lives as worthy of honour and respect. This applies to both sides of the same-sex marriage debate.

Supporters of same-sex marriage will point out the catastrophic moral failings of the various church leaderships when it comes to the protection of children. It's a fair assessment to make. However, it's not a full assessment of the contribution of the Christian church to the development of our land. On a daily basis, the churches educate hundreds of thousands of young Australians, care for thousands more in hospitals and lend a hand to people in need through their various charities and social activities. They have a right to be heard.

Equally, opponents of same-sex marriage should remember their silence and complicity as it relates to the treatment of gays and lesbians since the First Settlement. The church that was founded by a saviour who was *"he friend of publicans and sinners"* doesn't seem to be a friend of gays and lesbians. When church leaders question the capacity of gays and lesbians to have loving relationships of value, they are questioning the essence of their humanity.

Our challenge is to strengthen our common identity despite the differences.

The Australian identity is accepting and egalitarian. We believe that Jack is as good as his master – and Jill is as good as Jack. Our citizenship allows people to make their own choices about how to live, who to love and how to worship.

Our citizenship is grounded not only in the right of the individual, but also in the willingness of all of us to contribute to our country. Menzies described Australians as a nation of *"lifters not leaners"*. In recent years, that phrase has remerged in our national life, and some have argued that it is about dividing us into two different groups – something akin to 'bludgers' versus 'workers'. I don't accept that view. *"Lifters not leaners"* is about aspiration, and a yearning to contribute rather than to be supported.

We are all supported at some time in our lives – by families, by friends and at times, by government, but the purpose of that support is to help us get back on our feet and to help us through life's trials.

It's a concept no different from John F. Kennedy's invocation *"Ask not what your country can do for you; ask what you can do for your country."*

If we believe in a citizenship of mutual respect and personal responsibility, then we have to ask, why are we standing against a change in the marriage laws that allows any Australian to marry and to care for another?

If we believe in a country where any opportunity is available to anyone provided they work hard, how can we deny the opportunity of marriage to those who seek to live up to its precepts?

And how do we explain why we entrust our most significant national institutions into the hands of gay and lesbian high court judges, members of parliament, soldiers, sailors and aviators, but not allow the same people to share in the full benefits and responsibilities of citizenship?

As Martin Luther King said in a different context, *"When any society says that I cannot marry a certain person, society has cut off a segment of my freedom."*[34]

The inherent nature of citizenship is the belief that all our lives have the same moral worth, and if we recognise that our lives have the same moral worth, then we can also accept that our relationships are of the same worth.

The commonality of identity

After the 2013 election, I was given a peculiar responsibility. I had to oversee the development of the Prime Minister's Christmas Card.

For a Prime Minister, a Christmas card is more than a Christmas card. It's a way to make contact with the thousands of people he or she might interact with during the year. Tony Abbott's list (with accurate addresses and without double-ups) topped 4,000, and was sent to heads of state, ambassadors, colleagues, party officials, premiers, business leaders, community leaders, local Party members and staff, as well as old friends. It was a logistics exercise and, a diary exercise, and I was glad when the very last card left the office.

A few weeks after the 2013 election, I held my first meeting with the Department of Prime Minister and Cabinet (PM&C) to discuss the Christmas card. Midway through the meeting, a Departmental official cleared her throat and said *"Paul, we need to discuss the overtly religious nature of the card. It is not acceptable and it needs to change."*

I was taken aback. The card as it stood had a photo of the Abbott family and a Christmas greeting. *"What do you mean overtly religious?"* I asked.

"Paul, it says 'Merry Christmas and Happy New Year'. Many people aren't Christians, you know. What if someone is offended?"

My answer, which I was subsequently told ricocheted through the halls of 1 National Circuit (the home of PM&C) was, *"Well, if they are offended, they won't get another card. Tony Abbott is not a 'Happy Holidays' sort of guy, he's a 'Merry Christmas' guy."*

"Can we revisit this Paul?"

"No."

The idea that people can be offended by the fact that someone else has a different faith is nonsense. Christmas cards, like Christmas carols or nativity scenes, are not offensive, nor are greetings for Ramadan or Passover.

Our identities are made up of many parts. They include our religious beliefs, our sexuality, our political views and our customs, traditions and relationships. They need not be hidden and they shouldn't be hidden. They should be celebrated, because they reflect the essence of who we are. By celebrating our differences, rather than hiding them, we are demonstrating mutual respect.

The irony of most of the current 'identity politics' debates is that the protagonists on both sides share similar experiences when it comes to prejudice.

The American constitutional lawyer William Eskridge, argues that the elements of religious prejudice are similar to those of anti-gay prejudice. Our religious and sexual identities are *"physically invisible and morally polarising"*. The Christian and gay communities are both *'nomic'* communities that are bound from within by associations that result in the development of a common heritage. Even though every life is different, they have common identities that shape the way in which they see and interpret the world. These religious and sexual identities involve thought and action. In the debate over same-sex marriage, both claim their actions are synonymous with their deepest values – their beliefs in love, fidelity, marriage and a moral life.

Religious faith is no less an integral part of a person's identity than their sexuality. In the words of American constitutional law expert Professor Alan Brownstein:

> *"For serious believers, religion is one of the most self-defining and transformative decisions of human existence. Religious beliefs affect virtually all of the defining decisions of personhood. They influence whom we will marry and what that union represents, the birth of our children, our interactions with family members, the way we deal with death, the ethics of our professional conduct, and many other aspects of our lives. Almost any other individual decision pales in comparison to the serious commitment to religious faith."*[35]

The person of faith yearns to protect their soul and to be worthy of their faith and God. Mostly, this yearning produces a better world, but we have also seen that when this faith is driven by a fear of being 'contaminated' by the outside world, it can be destructive. But this is not unique to those of religious faith. All parts of our identity, if not kept in a semblance of balance, can distort our character.

The religious nut, the political fanatic, the obsessive sports fan and the hard-core activist, while reflecting our individuality, all seem to reflect an incomplete view of the world. Nevertheless, when brought together, our various identities (religious, sexual, ethnic, cultural, familial and national) become the essence of who we are.

In this, the libertarian, the person of faith and the gay and lesbian activist share a common view: the state should avoid stigmatising, burdening, or discouraging conduct that is central to personal identity. The state should only intervene if there are strong public policy reasons to do so.

Freedom is only freedom if we can confidently live out the various parts of our identity. Gays and lesbians learned a generation ago that freedom limited to the bedroom is not freedom, because identities are not just expressed in the privacy of our own home; they are expressed in the marketplace, the workplace and anywhere else where people meet and interact.

Likewise, people of faith do not want the expression of their faith to be limited to a church, mosque or synagogue, but to be lived out through lives of kindness and generosity expressed in their interactions with family, friends and colleagues.

Both Christians and gays have suffered from attempts to limit their identities. Gays and lesbians want freedom beyond the bedroom and people of faith want to express their faith beyond their church, mosque or synagogue. To all groups, conservatives should defend the right of people to live out their identities, because this is their authentic self.

The public should have room for all, even when those identities, at a superficial level, appear to be in conflict. Maybe it says something about us that two of the cultural phenomena that Sydney is known for are Hillsong and Mardi Gras. They both communicate the same message; in Australia, you can be free to be who you want to be.

Free speech means that we do not have to apologise for, lie about or hide our identities. The lesson of history is that when a state seeks to destroy an identity its legacy can be anger or a hardening of identity or a politicisation of a previously disorganised group. In the words of Eskridge, *"When the state makes it a crime to express oneself...the state is likely to embitter the objects of the suppression and to empower its own worst bigots"*.

One of the reasons why conservatives often argue against politically correct speech is because it simply pushes the view underground. The recent convulsions in the United States are a reflection of what happens when we seek to silence each other, rather than engage in dialogue.

Almost ten years ago, Columbia University in New York extended an invitation to the President of Iran, Mahmoud Ahmadinejad to speak. The move was attacked from both the left and the right. Ahmadinejad was anti-American, anti-women, anti-gay and anti-Jewish, and it was argued that he shouldn't be allowed to speak. However, the university refused to budge. Free speech was important and the students would get their chance to question the Iranian President.

When the day arrived, the President gave his address to a polite audience, and in the subsequent question and answer session he was asked about the plight of gays and lesbians in Iran. It was then that the wonder of free speech shone through.

Ahmadinejad said, *"In Iran, we don't have homosexuals, like you have in your country."*

After a moment of silence, the audience burst into laughter.

Ahmadinejad's worldview was only exposed because he was allowed to speak. However, before we laugh too loudly, we should remind ourselves that 'out of sight, out of mind' was also the approach in Australia some 40 or 50 years ago. Since that time, we have learned that people should be allowed to be their full selves, and it is a lesson that can still be applied to people of different identities today.

All people, in different ways, seek to navigate and synthesise the identities, relationships and loyalties that run through their lives. This means different things to different people. What does it mean to be an Australian if you are a Pentecostal trying to raise a family in the suburbs; or a Muslim woman who wears a hijab as she undertakes her liberal arts degree; or a gay tradie who volunteers with the RFS but still finds it difficult to make friends; or an Indigenous elder on a pension living in remote Australia; or a Catholic divorcee trying to see his children more than once a week?

We all must navigate our way through the conflicting expectations that are placed on us. Our challenge is to offer each other a hand as we navigate our own paths. Sexuality, faith, family, ethnicity and a secular culture make it easier for some, more than others. Nevertheless, our hope must be to develop lives that are authentic and that allow us to be comfortable in our own skin.

This requires all of us to have a broader view of what diversity means. We cannot allow a belief in diversity to be the acceptance of only some characteristics. Real diversity embraces people as we find them. When we speak about diversity – we aren't just referring to race or sexuality; we also mean Catholics and atheists, Jews and Hindus, millennials and baby boomers, conservatives and greens, bogans and hipsters. Diversity cannot simply accommodate one type of difference; it must accommodate all differences.

We must be able to lead lives that allow us to feel the gentle discomfort of difference. Interacting with people of different backgrounds is good for the soul. It puts a spotlight on our beliefs, and if we are adventurous, to question the assumptions on which we base our lives. It draws us into a bigger world where we meet, interact and rub shoulders with people with whom we don't necessarily agree.

During 2008, American liberals, particularly those studying on

American campuses, were in love with Barack Obama. To them, he was the greatest orator since Socrates, the most telegenic politician since Jack Kennedy and the greatest political intellect since the days when Thomas Jefferson dined alone.

I was studying at the Harvard Kennedy School at the time and called the unquestioning devotion 'cultish'. The members of the 'cult' weren't impressed. In response, I could have either railed against my minority status, or treated it for what it was: an opportunity to engage and grow in an environment where I was not part of the majority.

One should never have to hide one's identity, beliefs or worldview. To do that is to deny a small part of yourself. During that campaign and in the early days of the Obama presidency, I took a peculiar delight in wearing a t-shirt to class that had a smiling Barack Obama with Mickey Mouse ears (maybe it was my Australian aversion to authority shining through). Schools of government, like the Kennedy School, are built on debate, and in classes and study groups, I put the case that Obama was just a man like anyone else. He would face economic, institutional and social pressures just like every other president. In time, he would face choices and trade-offs that would make him disappoint those with unrealistic expectations.

It was to the credit of Harvard that it encouraged a culture that allowed such debate to thrive. The institution is accustomed to differences. Its students come from almost every part of the world, from every socio-economic background and from every religion, and yet it understands that you can create a shared culture out of many identities. It requires each identity, not to seek supremacy over the other, but to understand that they are part of a shared identity.

We live in a culture that seeks to eliminate our differences, but the truth is that differences are healthy, even if they can feel uncomfortable at times. Our differences allow us to explore our individuality, identity and worldview. They allow us to see the broader sweep of life, which in turn, can make our worldview clearer and sharper. This is freedom.

"*I am what I am*" is more than a progressive value, a libertarian ideal, or indeed, a conservative reflection of the image of God in man. It is a deep universal ideal that is in the hearts of all people.

Enlarging liberty

The paradox of liberty is that we often restrict liberty for some so that it is enlarged for others. Mostly, liberty is about trade-offs. The sum of law should result in more choice, more opportunity and more freedom than if we let mayhem reign or despots rule.

Freedom has a purpose; it allows us as individuals and as a community to lead good lives in which everyone has the opportunity to be who they want to be.

As yet, the case has not been put as to why limiting the freedom of gays and lesbians to marry increases the freedom available for heterosexuals.

Marriage is a private choice in a public sphere. Government regulates marriage because marriage is a foundational institution on which our community life is founded. Government has a vested interest in its success.

However, government has set limits that have clear public policy consequences. No one in our country disputes the wisdom of banning underage marriage. The reasons are compelling: there is not informed consent, psychological damage can be done, and children are not ready for the responsibilities of adulthood.

The reasons for the ban on marriage to close relatives are also clear. Besides the 'eeeekkkk' factor, there are three compelling reasons why marriage to close relatives is banned around the world. First, the science is clear; people with close genetic identities run great risks if they seek to have children. Second, it creates relationship ambiguity that is damaging psychologically. Third, it undermines the family if the relationship fails. For an unrelated couple, a divorce is a tragedy, but for a related couple, a divorce would be like taking a meat axe to the entire family unit.

While government has regulated the parameters of the civil contract of marriage, it is silent on the private conduct within marriage. Government does not prescribe what you or I should do in our bedrooms, how household duties are drawn up, or how often a husband or wife should visit the in-laws. Nor, in Western democracies, are married people fined or punished for adultery. Government is silent because these matters are in the private sphere. It recognises that, in the words of John Stuart Mill, *"over his own body and mind, the individual is sovereign"*.

However, it is ironic that many who resent the ever-encroaching zeal of government to control or know as much about our lives as possible, also argue that government should not allow gay, lesbian, transgender and intersex Australians the right to marry.

As the Liberal Democrat David Leyonhjelm reminds us, marriage *"is a private choice"*, and instead of trusting people to make the right choices for their lives, government seeks to intervene. For him, this is a matter that relates to our freedom:

> *"I support marriage equality because I think that people ought to have the freedom to choose their own life path.*
>
> *"When the law says that gay, lesbian, bisexual, trans, and intersex people cannot marry, in an important sense it is diminishing their liberty and their ability to make life plans: a major choice is closed off. The state is interfering, intervening, telling certain people that they can do what they want, except when they can't (while everyone else, of course, can)."*[86]

Giving gays and lesbians the right to marry the person they love will not limit the rights of anyone else. Sometimes, extending a right is akin to deciding how to cut a cake, – one person's larger slice coming at the expense of another. But that is not the case when it comes to expanding access to marriage.

Indeed, to strengthen another's life and to help them fulfil their potential will always benefit others. When the US Court of Appeal struck down a proposal to ban same-sex marriage in California, it argued that the ban *"...serves no purpose, has no effect, other than to lessen the status and dignity of gays and lesbians in California, and to officially reclassify their relationships and families as inferior to those of opposite-sex couples."*[87]

The Court went on to say:

> *"The name 'marriage' signifies the unique recognition that society gives to harmonious, loyal, enduring and intimate relationships.*
>
> *'The designation of 'marriage' is the status we recognise. It is the principal manner in which the State attaches respect and dignity to the highest form of committed relationship and to the individuals who have entered into it.'"*

By extending the liberty of others, we expand liberty for ourselves. Liberty always thrives when people are given respect and dignity, and when people are able to be their better selves.

Porous rights

It was John Howard who first used the term 'mutual responsibility'. He argued that those who receive unemployment benefits should make a contribution by working for them. The essence of 'mutual responsibility' is the relationship between the governed and the government. Our interactions with the laws of the land have a deep influence on how we see our country and our place within it. We seek fairness and consistency. Yet when it comes to modern marriage laws, fairness and consistency is missing.

A mass murderer in any Australian gaol can marry, as can a convicted wife basher or child molester, but an SAS soldier, or a policeman or an ambulance officer who happens to be gay or lesbian cannot.

A gay or lesbian Indigenous Australian can't marry in his or her homeland, but a gay or lesbian Australian with a British passport (or who has a partner with a British passport) can be married at the local British High Commission or a British Consulate. To date, hundreds of such ceremonies have occurred in embassies and high commissions across Australia, even if technically the law says they have not occurred on 'Australian soil'.

A heterosexual who has been legally divorced after his or her second, third or fourth marriage can marry, but a gay or lesbian who has been with their partner for 20, 30 or 40 years cannot.

A gay or lesbian Australian can fill out his or her Census form and note that it acknowledges gay marriage but he or she cannot avail themselves of that option.

A gay or lesbian couple can decide that they can't wait any longer and travel to New Zealand, the United Kingdom, the United States or elsewhere to get married, but in doing so, they marry away from most of their family and friends.

Since 2013, gay and lesbian Australians have been able to marry overseas. Under the Howard and Rudd Governments and throughout most of the Gillard Government, embassies and consulates were instructed not to issue Certificates of No Impediment to gays or lesbians. This is a certificate that countries ask for to prove that there are no legal impediments to a marriage (for example, the person is already married).

In any event, the decision to deny gays and lesbians a Certificate of No Impediment was honoured in the breach. Often, the local DFAT official would say, with a smile and wink to a male applying for the certificate would say *"I'm sure you are marrying a lovely girl."* The applicant would grin and say something like, *"It's going to be a beautiful wedding"*. The bad law was gamed, and no one felt guilty about it.

Already, thousands of gay and lesbian Australian couples have married overseas, including two members of the NSW Parliament.

However, this is still not complete recognition by Australia, with DFAT noting on its Smart Traveller website, *"Same-sex marriages conducted overseas are not recognised as a marriage in Australia, but may be evidence of a de facto relationship for the purposes of Commonwealth, State and Territory laws."*

We are now seeing a system develop whereby gay and lesbian couples are circumventing Australian law to get married. Mostly, they travel overseas and return to Australia as newlyweds. These couples have made their vows like any other married couple, they keep house and share their lives like a married couple, and they have been declared to be married by another nation, but when they return to Australia, their marriage is classified as a 'de facto relationship', effectively mocking the promises the couple made to each other and the lives that they lead.

The law is not keeping up with what is happening overseas, it is not keeping up with people's relationships and it is not keeping up with the actions of hundreds, if not thousands of Australians who are marrying under the laws of other jurisdictions.

The need for grace

Grace is a lost virtue in our public life and we are all the poorer for its loss.

The age of Twitter encourages us to pile on to mistakes, to question the virtue of others and to be outraged at the missteps of others. If the East Germans had had Twitter during the Cold War, they wouldn't have needed the Stazi. We have turned our public life into a pantomime where even the mere appearance of a political leader results in catcalls and boos. The end result is a polity where it is safer to argue for 'your base' than to engage in meaningful discourse. It takes grace to meet people where they are and to engage with their fears.

The same-sex marriage debate has been plagued by a willingness to think the worst of each other. We see Christians all too willing to question the morality of others, and we see supporters of same-sex marriage all too willing to shout down their opponents.

We see Christians proclaim a gospel without the sweetness of grace and we see progressives proclaim a mantra about embracing diversity – but it's only diversity for some. It's not diversity for Catholics, Presbyterians, Pentecostals, Baptists, Jews and Muslims.

Our challenge is to see each other as we are, to show the grace to accept differences, welcome strangers and meet people where they are.

One man who has a deep capacity for that at a personal level is Tony Abbott. He doesn't lose friends. While the wounds are still healing from the events of September 2015, I suspect that in time, after much water has passed under the bridge, old friends will become friends again.

I saw Tony's capacity for friendship come to the fore when Malcolm McGregor became Cate McGregor. Tony was then Opposition Leader, and McGregor had just published a book entitled *An Indian Summer of Cricket*, for which Tony agreed to write a review.

The staff didn't know he had agreed to this request, and one Sunday morning I received an email from Tony asking for feedback on the review he had written. As I read it, with a coffee in one hand

and my Blackberry in the other, I was astounded at the grace and wisdom Tony brought to the page. My reply was to the point: *"I have never felt prouder working for you."*

This is what he wrote. It is a testimony of what public life can be:

"While India's tour disintegrated, McGregor was coming apart too. As he writes in the last chapter, back in 1985 he'd been diagnosed as transgendered but had resolved, in his own words, to 'man up' and get on with life. Last summer, the strain of trying to be what, deep down, he was not became too much. Between the end of the series and finishing the book, faced with total personal collapse or a leap into the unknown, Malcolm has become Cate. Those who knew him will be shocked, McGregor writes, but not offended, she hopes.

Throughout the book, McGregor has wrestled with the impact of change on identity. Is the 20-over game the real thing, for instance? After some struggle, this instinctive traditionalist tentatively and at times reluctantly concludes that, yes, it is because enough of Test cricket's concentration, struggle and artistry have survived the translation. How much harder must it have been to deal with her own inner angst and to have concluded that change wasn't just unavoidable but desirable? All who have ever been on the precipice of changing their lives could benefit from another book from McGregor focusing on this, the biggest change imaginable.

How do institutions based on obedience to authority, respect for tradition and loyalty to comrades even survive, let alone flourish, in a world that's much more attuned to individual autonomy and authenticity? How do we encourage people to be selfless when we won't even let them be hard on themselves? These doubts, I suspect, stem from lack of sufficient faith in the power of our ideals and in our capacity to adapt. McGregor's life might actually be answering questions that the book merely poses.

With barely a blink, the army has accommodated her personal changes. After all, McGregor's professionalism and patriotism has not changed one bit, though much else have. Field Marshall Slim once remarked that moral courage is a higher and rarer virtue than physical bravery. *Army chief General David Morrison's launch of this book is a fitting salute to courage."*

Later when Abbott was Prime Minister, McGregor said, *"I did him a disservice and grossly underestimated his capacity for friendship. He embraced risk in doing that."* Tony, she said, had provided real leadership in recognising her as a transgender woman, but had received *"almost no credit"*. She went on to state:

> *"I find the reluctance of some in the human rights and gender lobbies to acknowledge exactly what Tony Abbott did quite puzzling. Some people really need to know how to take yes for an answer."*

We also need grace in the way in which we approach issues, and this can be just as difficult.

Rodney Croome faced such a moment in late 2015 following the decision by a Tasmanian same-sex marriage activist to take the local Catholic archbishop to the Anti-Discrimination Commission.

Rodney has been arguing for the rights of gay, lesbian, bisexual, transgender and intersex people for a quarter of a century. His work has been recognised by an Order of Australia and in 2015 he was a finalist for Australian of the Year.

When homosexuality was a crime in Tasmania, punishable by 25 years gaol, Rodney and his partner took the state to the United Nations (UN). At the time, I was one of those Australians who was angered by his actions – taking Australia to the UN seemed un-Australian. With the passage of time, I realise that Rodney had a better idea of what it meant to be Australian than I did. He used his rights as a citizen to argue for change. That is what free speech is all about. It is free speech that allows the unorthodox to become orthodox. Free speech creates the environment for continual, gradual change.

In late 2015, Rodney wrote a piece calling for both sides of the same-sex marriage debate to respect each other's rights. He wrote the piece failing attempts to ban a publication distributed by the Archbishop of Hobart entitled *"Don't Mess with Marriage"*. Rodney recognised that the complaint made against the Archbishop was an own goal that detracted from the compelling and positive message of those seeking change.

The *"Don't Mess with Marriage"* booklet was, well, how do I put it, boring. It had the excitement of a leaflet offering a funeral plan or trying to sell a residence in a retirement village. In political terms, it had no cut through at all.

However, the complaint against the Archbishop galvanised support around him. Even if you disagreed with the case put by the booklet, people respected the right of the Archbishop to articulate the tenets of his faith.

It was in this setting that Croome reminded his supporters of their own responsibility to be part of a respectful debate. He wrote:

> *"If free speech is hampered during a plebiscite campaign the outcome risks being de-legitimised.*
> *"The outcome will also be tarnished if ordinary Australians are hurt, harmed and turned off by the debate.*
> *"In sum, the task before us is to strike a balance between free speech and social responsibility that both sides can stick to despite the pressures of a national vote.*[38]*"*

In some ways, Rodney's actions took as much courage as his actions some 20 years earlier. Calling on your opponents to change is easy, but asking your own supporters to change is a true act of leadership.

There was blowback from his supporters. He was roundly criticised on his Facebook page. However, the reaction challenged me as well.

The criticisms were made by people who had experienced discrimination, who had lived during a time when their sexuality was effectively a 'criminal offence', or who had been denied jobs because of their sexuality, and who at times, had been denied the love and support of family and friends. To them, the people who oppose same-sex marriage today are the same people who opposed attempts to decriminalise homosexuality a generation ago.

Showing grace to opponents is not an easy ask, but it is essential if we are to protect Australia from the tares and turmoil of other countries.

In this debate, it will require an informal network on both sides to keep the debate on an even path. This will not stymie free speech, but rather protect it from the excesses of those whose anger overrides their reason.

4

TRADITION AND CHANGE

"We live not only our own lives but, whether we know it or not, also the life of our times"
- Laurence Van Den Post.

My father's family was a typical white, working class, Catholic family, from the inner suburbs of Sydney. My grandfather, too young to enlist in the Great War and too old to enlist in the Second World War, was a deckhand on the Manly ferry for fifty years while my grandmother stayed at home and raised a family. They had five children, a large family by today's standards, but not in those times.

My mother's family lived in the inner west of Sydney. In those days, it had not been yuppified or filled with expensive new apartments. My pop had served in the Navy during the Second World War, and my grandmother waited for him to safely return, as she did for all seven of her brothers. However, two of her brothers did not return; they were killed when the Japanese sunk a hospital ship. They lived normal lives, saw nothing unusual in sending every son to war, but were, in hindsight, extraordinary. Unlike, my father's family, my mother's family was not overly religious, but they were Anglican, and it was part of their identity.

My mother and father's families were, for all intents and purposes, homogenous. They were Australian, white, working class, Labor supporters, but they did not readily identify with each other, because their religious denominations were different.

Such were the times, which saw the same religious conflict cut across every part of our national life. Even our national cricket team was split down religious lines, with one of our greatest bowlers, Bill O'Reilly, who was a Catholic, having little to do with our greatest batsman, Don Bradman.

Homogeneity was seen as a way of keeping families strong. You married similar people, you married within the same race, the same social class and the same religious denomination.

In keeping with the times, my father's Catholic siblings married people from similar backgrounds. My father broke with tradition by marrying an Anglican (or as it was called back then, Church of England). My mother was warned about the dangers of marrying a Catholic, but eventually my parents married, and over time Dad became a loved member of my mother's family.

My father's brothers and sisters are now in their seventies, eighties and nineties. None of them ever divorced and between them they produced 21 grandchildren (and dozens of great-grandchildren).

And this is where the story of my family changed. Included in these families you will now find Catholics, Anglicans, Buddhists, Muslims and Pentecostals. The grandchildren have married spouses who are Arab, Vietnamese, Italian and English.

There is a smattering of family members with different sexualities, plenty of Liberal voters and even a few Greens as well (I'm still gobsmacked by that!). The grandchildren and great grandchildren of a man and a woman who never left Australia can now be found in Thailand, Saudi Arabia, the United States and throughout their homeland.

Here is the wonder. This family tree that started with one family has now spread its branches far and wide, and those branches are all strong. The differences have not weakened us; instead, they are a source of celebration.

Like all families, this extended family has its ups and downs, but we stay in contact at christenings, anniversaries and weddings, and we read about each other's lives on Facebook. We inquire after those who fall ill, quietly share gossip when life's circumstances change and mourn and reminisce when one of us 'slips the surly bonds of Earth'. Our family is as joyous, functional and rambunctious as any other.

If my grandparents, Evelyn and Donald, could see this family that is their legacy, I think they'd marvel at what has become bigger, stronger and so different from anything they could ever have imagined.

Some of the assumptions that my grandparents' generation held to be truths about marriage and families have not withstood the test of time. The strength of families did not lie in a common race or religion or social bond; rather, we realised that the strength of our families came from the knitting together of heart and soul, of the stories and experiences we shared and the common history that is ours.

If there is a lesson from the changing state of marriage and families, it is that we are all the product of our times. Every generation seeks to make sense of the world by the learned truths that we hold and the experiences that we share.

Conservatives and tradition

Almost 150 years ago, John Stuart Mill, a man who could be called one of the world's earliest feminists, wrote an essay entitled *The Subjection of Women*. While he was reflecting on the economic forces shaping the lives of women, his words speak to all of us about the forces that shape our lives:

> '*What is the peculiar character of the modern world — the difference which chiefly distinguishes modern institutions, modern life itself, from*

those of times long past? It is, that human beings are no longer born to their place in life, and chained down by an inexorable bond to the place they are born to, but are free to employ their faculties, and such favourable chances as offer, to achieve the lot which may appear to them most desirable.[39]"

Understanding change is at the heart of the conservative temperament. As the father of conservatism, Edmund Burke wrote in his defining work, *Reflections on the Revolution in France*:

"Instead of casting away all our old prejudices, we cherish them to a very considerable degree, and, to take more shame to ourselves, we cherish them because they are prejudices; and the longer they have lasted, and the more generally they have prevailed, the more we cherish them. We are afraid to put men to live and trade each on his own private stock of reason; because we suspect that this stock in each man is small, and that the individuals would do better to avail themselves of the general bank and capital of nations, and of ages.[40]"

But Burke was not arguing for institutions to be left alone. To only look back is to become like Lot's wife, frozen in time and lost to the present. Indeed, to leave an institution alone, to ignore change, is to leave it to wither. Then, it is susceptible to violent upheaval. By then, the institution has become incapable of change and is irrelevant. In other words, those who seek to freeze institutions in time weaken the very institutions they seek to protect.

Still, the question of change forces us to question ourselves about what we believe, What is ephemeral? What must be preserved? What is just habit? What must be left behind?

The conservative answers this not with belligerence but with reflection. Conservatives understand that the energy of constant change, which enables modern economies and societies to thrive and bounce back after setbacks, is only possible within a framework of rules, customs, laws and institutions.

It will always be to the benefit of Australia that Sir Robert Menzies created a Liberal Party based on liberal and conservative wings – because tradition and change work best together. The party he created is conservative in temperament, but liberal in outlook.

He understood that humanity is not meant to be the blind servant of institutions, and institutions are meant to serve people. Institutions and traditions are not meant to enslave us to the past, or to the powerful few who control them; rather, they are meant to be the source of our rights and the foundation of our freedom.

True conservatism is a temperament. It has a quiet dignity that carries people with it because it knows that it is the social fabric that binds us together. To mock my neighbour, to decry his values, is ultimately to weaken myself.

It is a philosophy grounded in humility, because the conservative tradition understands that humanity is frailer than we like to imagine or care to admit. We see our lives for what they are – fragile and all too short.

We know that mostly, our hopes, our loves, our losses and our very lives are not ours to control. At times, this makes us cling to the past when we should loosen our grip, forgo change when we ought to embrace it or clutch to a certainty when we might let it go, because we know that the future is not assured.

This understanding of human frailty recognises that mostly, we are made stronger by tradition, convention and institutions, which are the embodiment of centuries of human wisdom. Friedrich Hayek, the classical liberal philosopher, argued that this wisdom, in its totality, contains a sum of understanding that a person could not learn or assimilate in a lifetime. Implicit in this wisdom is the recognition that it has evolved. Its survival is the proof of the logic embedded in it, and reminds us there is more to life than rationality, and that for all we know, there is even more that we don't.

George H.W. Bush summed it up best in a diary entry he made during his presidency; *"The longer I'm in this job, the more I think that prudence is a value, and I hope experience matters."*[41] He saw that overreach is often as dangerous as inaction. To him, the goal of politics was to do *"the most good I can and the least harm."* My experience with Tony Abbott is that this best summarised his instinctive approach to the prime ministership. Unlike his predecessors, Abbott had no lofty view of his own abilities that blinded him to the possibility that his good intentions could result in harm. This realisation strengthened his judgment rather than weakened it.

Conservatives know their own fallibility. The conservative temperament is humble. It does not have the stridency and the certainty of its opponents. The conservative thinks carefully, walks gently and reaches out to test his or her arguments. When he or she is convinced, then and only then does he or she act for the greater good.

The conservative temperament has taught us that change is more beneficial when it is continual and gradual rather than abrupt, and when it respects the past rather than rejects it.

In the words of Andrew Sullivan, *"All conservatism begins with loss. If we never knew loss, we would never feel the need to conserve."*[42] This nostalgic temperament has at its heart the memory of human experience. We know we are not any better than previous generations, for we stand on others' achievements. We mourn the little losses – the library that has closed, the suburb that has been levelled for an airport, the football team that no longer takes the field, and the churches that lie empty, knowing that something of our collective memory is lost with them.

Yet we also take joy from continuity and the traditions that remind us of our history and the body of people to which we belong. It is this temperament that infuses Australian liberalism. True liberalism, rather than its modern American cousin 'progressive-ism', is about the rights of all to be treated fairly and to be ascribed due process. It does not seek the dominance of one worldview over another or one religion over another. Rather, it is human freedom and the broadening of human endeavour, in all its forms, that is at the centre of our liberalism.

Menzies recognised that the weakness of traditional liberalism is that it mistakes the neutrality of the state for a disinterested nonchalance as some groups seek to assert themselves over others. It is why, in some parts of the world, modern liberals struggle to call out radical extremism, but conservatives do and will. It is why, in parts of Europe, minorities such as gays and lesbians, Jews and Christians are supporting conservative causes, because they will stand in the breach against extremists.

Menzies' liberalism draws together the coherent truths of the liberal and conservative philosophies. As the liberal believes in the rights of the individual, the conservative believes that properly constituted institutions should be the foundation of rights. The conservative recognises that our freedom does not sit on its own, but is embodied in our institutions – the Crown, the Parliament and the Courts, and it lives and breathes in our churches and community institutions and in our communities and families.

To tear down an institution is to tear down the architecture of human freedom. Thus, the Australian liberals' philosophy is a belief in freedom underpinned by values; it is liberalism with guiding values.

It is through this lens of tradition and change, of individual freedom and guiding values, that we reflect on the issue of same-sex marriage.

Conservatives also believe that people, through institutions and social inducements, are capable of leading better lives. Marriage is one of the institutions that provides for this and there is no reason to believe that it will not do the same for gays and lesbians.

Because marriage is at the centre of our civilisation, conservatives fear that changes to marriage could result in detrimental changes to our way of life. It is a fair argument, but one that can be answered by looking at history, at international experience and the evolution of marriage as it relates to anthropology, law, sociology, economics and literature.

While many say that marriage is an unchanging institution, the reality is that this claim is untrue. Marriage gently evolves with every generation. In the words of E. J. Graff, *"Marriage has always been a social battlefield, its rules constantly shifting to fit each culture and class, each era and economy."*[43]

Some feminists have argued that marriage was created for subordinating men to women. However, it appears from the earliest times that marriage sought to deal with the worst excesses of men who could father a child but then refuse to support the woman or child. Marriage tied men to women. It created the moral structures whereby men honoured their commitments to women and to the children they helped create.

A man could not walk out and leave a mum and kids without feeling the stigma of having not fulfilled his primary responsibility to the community and society. Marriage ensured that men fulfilled their moral, physical and financial duties to care for their families.

Over the centuries, marriage has evolved. Even over the past 55 years it has changed remarkably. Since the Commonwealth Marriage Act became law in 1961 it has been amended no less than 20 times. It was amended in 1966, 1973 (twice), 1976, 1982, 1985, 1988, 1990, 1991, 1992, 1994, 1995, 1996, 1999, 2000, 2001, 2002, 2004, 2010 and 2011.

Marriage has evolved through time. No longer is the marriage contract negotiated in a notary's office (although we might say there is an exception with modern pre-nuptial agreements), nor is it considered an economic treaty or agreement between families or countries that treats their sons and daughters as though they were property.

In our society, no longer are young women and young men subject to arranged marriages; no longer are people of different races banned from marrying; no longer are Aboriginals required to seek permission from white authorities to marry; no longer are people with disabilities prevented from marrying; no longer are married women banned from owning property in their own name; no longer is it claimed that marital rape is not a crime; no longer are women denied the right to see their children following divorce proceedings; no longer are prisoners denied the right to marry; no longer are parties in a divorce required to prove who is 'at fault'; no longer do we keep slaves who are prohibited from marrying; and no longer are kings required to abdicate if they seek to marry a divorced woman.

Marriage has evolved with the society it serves. Change is mostly incremental and generally lags the spirit of the times. It is in our homes and communities that changes are first tested and argued. Without exception, changes that we take for granted today were hotly contested in their time. Initially, change is always seen as unnatural, and as a disruption of and an offence against the natural order. Indeed, the arguments about time-honoured traditions were used against our ancestors when they sought to make changes in their own times.

Most often, the politicians of the day seek to 'protect' marriage from people or groups who are 'immature' or not suited to making one of life's most important decisions. Indeed, centuries ago, it was argued that only parents were responsible enough to choose the spouse of their children. With every change there is concern that it represents a threat to families and that the family unit will not survive.

Since the earliest days of the First Settlement, when authorities had to consider whether convicts should be allowed to marry, governments (of all persuasions) have argued that people can't be trusted to marry, that certain groups should keep to themselves and not weaken 'the races' or the institution, and that government restrictions on marriage have the welfare of children at heart.

It was argued that you couldn't trust women to make decisions on their own; you couldn't trust convicts to settle down; you couldn't trust Aboriginals to make sense of a white man's institution; and you couldn't break the laws of God by allowing the races to intermarry. Ironically, all of this was argued during a time when children as young as 12 or 14 (depending on the state) were allowed to marry.

The truth was that in disallowing so many groups to marry, we denied them the capacity to love more fully, to selflessly give to and take responsibility for another, and to nurture and love children.

We should ask ourselves, who benefited from stopping Aboriginals marrying each other or non-Aboriginal people? Who benefited from stopping Australian soldiers from returning to Australia with Japanese wives at the end of the Second World War? Who benefited when a disabled person found someone to love and we denied them that love? Who benefited from trying to stop convicts setting up homes and making honest lives?

And in current times, who benefits from stopping a gay member of the ADF from marrying? Who benefits when a young lesbian can only get married overseas and not in her homeland? Who benefits when a transgender person is forced to divorce the only person who truly accepts them because that's what the law requires if you want to change the gender on your birth certificate?

Conservatives respect the fragility of life. None of us knows the paths that our lives will take, the unexpected challenges and tragedies we will face, or the inexplicable mistakes we will make. But we know it will be easier with the support of a spouse, children and loved ones. Extending marriage to gay, lesbian, transgender and intersex people is about giving them the same opportunity for support that all other Australians have.

The lesson of history is that marriage follows the times. It changes incrementally. Instead of growing weaker, it grows stronger. Instead of being consigned to irrelevancy, the institution evolves to reflect the times. It is this evolution that strengthens the institution and ensures that it remains relevant.

The evolution of marriage

> *"Husbands, love your wives, as Christ loved the church and gave himself up for her... Husbands ought to love their wives as their own bodies. He who loves his wife, loves himself."*
> - Ephesians 5:25

The above verse is read at many weddings. It sounds warm and pleasant, and the invocation cannot offend anyone. But in its day, St Paul's clarion call was revolutionary. It was a time when women were not considered the equals of men, but the possessions of men. Polygamy, concubines and easy divorce meant that women were peripheral to the lives of men. They could be discarded at little cost.

The church had a different vision of marriage. It believed in monogamy. The idea that men were limited to one wife was, in its time, a social revolution. It meant the elevation of women and fairer treatment than they had previously received.

No longer could the rich walk away from private promises of

fidelity. The church taught that marriage was not disposable, because people shouldn't be disposable. It was a leveller, with rich and poor making the same promises. The promises were not just made to another person, they were promises made before God. No longer just a matter of law, they were now matters of soul.

However, the church meandered through the first millennium after Christ without a defined doctrine on marriage. It was not until the 12th century that the Church made marriage a sacrament. According to the Catechism of the Catholic Church sacraments are *"efficacious signs of grace, instituted by Christ and entrusted to the Church, by which divine life is 'dispensed' to us"*. It was during the Council of Trent (1545 – 1563) that marriage was defined as *"the conjugal union of man and woman, contracted between two qualified persons, which obligates them to live together for life."*

It was the church that ended the private promises of marriage and made it a community ritual. All too often, men made promises of lifelong devotion in a moment of passion or manipulation and then walked away. Inevitably, these became *'he said/she said'* disputes. The ecclesiastical authorities realised that the promise of lifelong devotion and the sexual union of the couple were private acts, and that marriage needed a public or community component. Marriages needed a witness, and the private promise was required to be made publicly.

Vows became something that should be exchanged *in facie, Ecclesiae* – in the presence of the congregation. While public commitments are accepted as a given today, this was an innovation that was neither welcomed nor applauded in its time. For congregations, it seemed like another church imposition, and it took generations for the church wedding to take hold.

Following the French Revolution, the French took formal recognition of marriage further by insisting that marriages were a matter for the state, and that it was the civil recognition of marriage that made them legal.

In time, the English would regulate marriage as well, and it became both a civil right and a religious freedom. Marriage as an institution was thus born. Marriage became a demonstration of the authority of the state, and religious marriage became a reflection of religious freedom.

This is our inheritance: the right given by the state to marry the one you love, and the right of religions to solemnise marriage according to their teachings.

Thus marriage evolved from a private promise between a man and a woman to a public act, backed by the authority of the state and, for those who believed, given under the blessing of the church. But marriage was not for everyone.

Marriage and slaves

Slavery was part of the English way of life until 1833 and part of American life until the end of the Civil War in 1865. Men and women, by virtue of their colour, were kept as property. It was the political, social and, in the case of the United States, military battle of its day. The Christian church mostly sided with the abolitionists. In the words of St Paul, *"there is neither Jew nor Gentile, neither slave nor free, nor is there male and female, for you are all one in Christ Jesus."*

Slaves could not and did not legally marry. They were subject to the authority of their owner. Marriage would have mocked the foundational belief that slaves were property. They were denied the right to marry because implicitly they were not considered to be fully human. As the Chief Justice of the Supreme Court of North Carolina put it in the case of *Howard v Howard* in 1858, "*The relation of 'man and* wife' cannot exist among slaves. It is excluded, both on account of their incapacity to contract, and of the paramount right of ownership in them, as property."

Though the law might have owned a man or woman's body, it could never own a soul. Slaves made promises to each other, they made love and their promises were affirmed in private ceremonies, often held before other slaves. Often there was a deep pathos in the marriage ceremony, with ministers declaring *"until death or distance do you part."* In other words, if you were sold and sent away, the marriage would be no more. It was a world away from the declaration of Jesus, *"What therefore God hath joined together, let not man put asunder."*

To the courts and slave owners, these were not considered marriages. To them, the slaves were not married because the law did not allow it. While the slaves had sexual impulses, it was believed they should not be able to marry because they were incapable of forming the deep bonds of kinship and devotion that marriage requires. It sounds awfully familiar.

Marriage and love

Marriage in the 18th and 19th centuries was still fundamentally different to how we currently know it. Marriage was not about love in the romantic way in which we idealise it today. First and foremost, marriage was about economic security. Some might have been fortunate to experience physical attraction and to develop the love that comes from familiarity, but mostly, marriage was about securing your future and the future of your family. The historian Barbara Hanawalt said of the times, *"marriage for love has traditionally been assumed to be the dubious privilege of those without property"*.

There was no way to hide it. Marriage was all about money. As the English proverb from the 1600s says *"Who marrieth for love without money hath good nights and sorry days."* But that is not to say that the natural yearnings did not matter; instead, they became quantified. Daughters were traded like football players in a draft, with age, looks and skills implicitly monetarised.

At times, there were arbitrary attempts to change this market that operated between families. Florence tried to enforce a cap on dowries. However, the Medicis, who literally created the dollar symbol, removed the cap. In an argument that would do the Institute of Public Affairs proud, they stated that *"marriages must be free, and everyone should be free to endow his daughters, sisters and other female relatives as he sees fit and as he likes, because one must be able to arrange his affairs in this way."*

It is not surprising that the expressed outcome of such a system was that married women were considered to be the property of their husbands. The 18th century jurist Lord Blackstone put the legal position of wives in this way: *"In law husband and wife are one person, and that person is the husband.*[44]*"* It is why my grandparents often received letters addressed to "Mrs and Mrs Donald Ritchie", because by law and custom, they were considered to be one entity, personified by the name of the husband.

Effectively, Lord Blackstone was saying that a married woman's rights are derived from those of her husband. He is the sun and she is the moon. Wealth, security and the right to own property are only found in him. The wife is as much the husband's property as the cattle he owns.

But society works things out. The stern, male-centric view of marriage held by Lord Blackstone was a brittle creation. It meant that married women had fewer rights than single women. To use Lord Blackstone's analogy, in law, the single woman is one person and she embodies the rights of that person.

The Blackstone ideal was a disaster for women who married bad men. If a woman married a deadbeat, she was liable for his debts, but he could claim her assets, even if he walked out on her. Worse still, she had no right to care for her children, because in Blackstone's world a mother "*was entitled to no power but only to reverence and respect.*" As any parent knows, if you have no power, your children will not give you reverence and respect.

Blackstone's view of a mother's right to claim custody of her children was little different from that of the legislator who said that allowing women custody of children would "*weaken the ties of marriage by forcing both sexes into an unnatural antagonism*".

However, we should not be too harsh on Blackstone. He was, like all of us, the product of his times. In the past, we have seen history through the lens of the 'great man' who makes the world a better place. More recently, we have come to realise that all men and women are a mix of good and bad, both selfish and selfless, and capable of heroism as well as folly. But we should ask why Blackstone couldn't see the just needs of the women who appeared before him? Why could he not see the social changes occurring around him? Blackstone thought he was upholding the values of the time, of his faith, and protecting his country from the corroding forces of change. His motives were right, but history has judged him to be wrong.

In every generation, change to marriage is resisted. Changes to marriage are inevitably seen as an attack on marriage. As marriage is seen as an institution created by God, those who seek to change marriage are seen to be attacking God. In 1844, New York changed its law to allow women to own property in their own name. The move was roundly attacked. One legislator said it would result in "*infidelity in the marriage bed, a high rate of divorce and increased female criminality.*" When a similar law was proposed in London, *The Times* thundered that such measures would "*abolish families in the old sense.*"

In a sense, both the legislator and *The Times* were right to argue that giving women economic rights would result in an increase in divorce. Legal rights for women, including wives, loosened the economic chains that bound them. It meant that unmarried women were not consigned to poverty because they could not own property in their own right. Married women trapped in a heartless or cruel marriage, because the economic alternatives were too dreadful to imagine were starting to be given alternatives. Slowly, beneath the feet of men, a shift from servitude to partnership was occurring.

In 1857, the Matrimonial Causes Act was passed to allow civil courts rather than ecclesiastical courts to rule in relation to divorce and require ex-husbands to pay maintenance. The Act widened the availability of divorce and created the world's first family court. After all, why should a deserted wife need to appear in a court stuck between a murderer and a robber? Again, these changes to marriage were vigorously opposed.

It was argued that giving women rights, even the right to leave someone who was cruelly mistreating her, would be a threat to marriage. Giving women independence and security would strike at the heart of manhood – in the same way, no doubt, in which giving gay couples security under the law would strike at the heart of heterosexuality.

For most of human history, the expectation of marriage was economic security and companionship, rather than romantic love or sexual pleasure. That changed during the 19th century.

The 1866 description of marriage written by Lord Penzance in a court judgment caught the change: *"Marriage as understood in Christendom is the voluntary union for life of one man and one woman, to the exclusion of all others."* If the words sound familiar, it is because this definition was at the heart of the Howard Government's changes to marriage that were proclaimed in 2004. Explicit in Penzance's words is the concept of a partnership between a man and a woman. The generational change is captured in the movie *Titanic* when Rose is required to marry to secure the financial fortune of her family, but instead yearns for a life of love.

The changes that occurred to marriage were driven by the yearnings of women (as well as men) to make their own decisions, ones that reflected the nature of their lives. No longer were parents choosing a spouse for their children, nor were they being married off for money. The bonds of authority over women and men were loosening.

After millennia in the dark, people were walking out into the light and making more choices for themselves. They might have considered their lives to be preordained spiritually, but that did not mean they were bound to their farm, their trade or their lot in life. To use the Australian vernacular, they could '*have a go*'.

This changed decisions about marriage. It was now not about economy, but about heart, affection, attraction and choice. In the past, love sprung from years and decades together, sharing a path with its small triumphs and failures. In the new world, love could be found before marriage. It could be the certain foundation of a marriage rather than the potential result of one.

One of the ideas that conservatives are instinctively drawn to is that earlier times were better times. However, it is wrong to assume that the standards of the Victorian era created better people or higher standards. People were not that different centuries ago from what they are today. Love, passion and lust were as much a part of their inner lives as they are today. For example in pre-Victorian times, it was estimated that one in three conceptions in England occurred out of wedlock.

Though marriage was changing and society was witnessing the

advent of marriage for love, the institution had become a bulwark against those who did not join it. While marriage stood for love and lifelong commitment, there was harshness towards those who were outside of it or who did not conform to it. Unmarried adults were socially suspect, divorce carried a deep social stigma and access to the sacraments and the life of the church was denied to those whose morality was considered questionable.

This is best seen by the abdication crisis of 1936. King Edward VIII fell in love with a woman who was twice divorced. The relationship was a scandal, for it was unimaginable for a king, who was also head of the Church of England, to marry a commoner – and a divorced one at that. Two generations later, the heir to the throne would do just that. While the Prince of Wales had to marry in a civil ceremony at the local Guildhall, his marriage was subsequently blessed in a ceremony at St George's Chapel.

In its own way, the monarchy was changing with the times. Unlike in 1936, there was no constitutional crisis, there were no threats that the government would fall, or that the Commonwealth would dissolve. Life went on as normal, the crowds outside the guildhall cheered the newlyweds and the monarchy, like all healthy institutions, continued its evolution.

Again, we witnessed quiet, peaceful change. What we had held to be immutable was discovered to be malleable. The monarchy, one of the oldest institutions in the world, recognised that society no longer disqualifies people because of who they choose to love.

This value was reflected again in 2015 when changes to the Act of Succession were passed by parliaments across the British Commonwealth. The Act allows for the Sovereign to veto the marriage choice of the first six royals in line to the throne. However, if the Sovereign agrees to the marriage, the couple can be married under the UK Marriage Act.

The UK Marriage Act allows for same-sex marriage. In other words, Australian law allows for a future king or queen of Australia to marry their same-sex partner. If that day ever occurs, there will be coins minted, stamps commemorating the wedding produced by the Post Office and a worldwide TV audience tuning in.

My understanding of conservatives and progressives tells me that most republicans support same-sex marriage and many monarchists do not. If this is the case, this willingness of the royal family to allow same-sex marriages within their family must confound republicans and monarchists alike.

The King or Queen of Australia, though he or she may reside in the United Kingdom, is, by law, one of us. Without debating the merits of monarchy, I wonder how we have arrived at the situation where this ancient institution is ahead of Australian law when it comes to marriage? Or is it just that we are lagging the Anglosphere?

The changes that have occurred to marriage also reflect changes to our society. Over the past two centuries, we have witnessed an unravelling of old hierarchies that demanded unquestioned loyalty and obedience. In that world, the children obeyed the parents, the wife obeyed the husband, the slaved obeyed the master, the master obeyed the local authorities, the local authorities obeyed the King (and in some cases, the Pope) and the King obeyed God. The essence of a social system based on authority is that it relies on the goodness of men – even though, all too often, goodness is not found.

The challenge for conservatives is to preserve and strengthen the essential ingredients of the ties that bind. Conservatives do not demand loyalty, nor should we expect blind obedience to be the sustaining power of institutions. Loyalty and love must be freely given rather than demanded as a due. It is in this context that marriage, including same-sex marriage, is an essential foundation whereby individuals give themselves to something bigger than themselves – they give themselves to another and they give themselves to family. It is in marriage that the individual knits himself or herself to another individual and another family; and families are the foundation of communities, which are the heart and soul of countries.

Marriage and race

Mid-way through the 20th century most countries faced calls to overturn marriage bans between people of different races.

Australia had direct and indirect bans on inter-racial marriages that hindered the rights of people to marry the person they loved. The 'White Australia' policy, limitations on Aboriginals marrying, and strong community sentiment, all served to limit inter-racial marriages in Australia.

In the United States, two dozen American states had legal bans on interracial marriage in the mid-1950s. However, the advent of the Civil Rights Movement and a broader community debate on race saw the number of US states with bans on interracial marriage drop to 16 by 1967. That same year, the US Supreme Court ruled that bans on interracial marriages were unconstitutional.

In its day, interracial marriage frightened many white Americans because it struck at the core of American racial policies. As E. J. Graff put it, *"social equality wasn't frightening because it led to intermarriage; rather, intermarriage was frightening because it implied social equality."*

This was not a popular decision of the Supreme Court. According to the polling company Gallup, 72 per cent of Americans disapproved of inter-racial marriage and an astonishing 48 per cent believed it should be a crime. Gallop has kept track of this issue and by 2013, public approval for interracial marriage had risen to 87 per cent.[45]

On an issue that once generated heat, passion, anger and violence, we have witnessed a remarkable turnaround in half a century. While there is strong support among all age groups, there is a noticeable difference between generations – 96 per cent of 14-29 year olds approve of interracial marriage compared with 70 per cent of people over 65 years of age.

Over time, the change in attitudes was reflected in a change in the makeup of American families. According to the latest Census data from the United States, 16 per cent of marriages are interracial with 9 per cent of whites, 17 per cent of African Americans, 26 per cent of Hispanics and 28 per cent of Asians marrying someone of a different race.

One group that can take credit for the change in attitudes towards inter-racial marriage in the United States is the Catholic Church. The Church consistently opposed the ban on interracial marriage. In doing so, the Church lived out its gospel values.

Marriage and international precedent

For the past 15 years, we have witnessed a movement across Western nations to allow same-sex marriage.

In the countries that my old boss Tony Abbott calls *"our cousins"*, namely, New Zealand, the United Kingdom and Canada, same-sex marriage is now law. In the United States, our strategic partner, it is legal in all 50 states.

Other countries that have legalised same-sex marriage include Ireland, Netherlands, Belgium, Spain, South Africa, Norway, Colombia, Sweden, Portugal, Iceland, Argentina, Uruguay, France, Brazil, Luxembourg, Denmark, Portugal, Finland, and parts of Mexico.

In changing an institution, conservatives fear unforeseen consequences. We understand that to discard or change a tradition or institution can impact others. It is akin to losing a tooth and finding that the loss of one tooth loosens or moves the teeth around it.

The evidence is that legalising same-sex marriage has not had negative consequences. The unforeseen consequence has been that people from Ireland, the United States and elsewhere say they feel prouder about their country. There are no movements back. The cultural wars that existed in countries that embraced same-sex marriage have not intensified. Instead, they have dissipated. Everyone has moved on.

Marriage and divorce

If people kept their word, there would be no need for marriage and no need for divorce. Marriage binds us to our promise to love and care for another all the days of our life.

However, the sum of human experience has shown us that people break promises. Rules for marriage and divorce are necessary because they bring justice and mercy to our personal commitments to others.

Our family law system is about fairness. It protects the wife of 30 years who supported a husband through law school and raised three children, it protects the young mother who is seeking to escape an abusive husband and it watches over the interests of children when the enmity between two parents becomes destructive.

Family law weighs up our contributions, sacrifices and failings to ensure there is justice when a conflict appears irreconcilable. Because marriage is fundamental to society, it has an interest in ensuring that disputes are settled justly. If there was no justice in marriage it would weaken the attractiveness of marriage and weaken it as an institution.

If the rules are clear, and fairness is seen to be there, then couples can have confidence that they will be supported if their marriage does not go the distance.

In the 1840s, Mary Gove Nichols left the husband who beat her. She sought from the courts the right to contact her children but she lost. Later, she and her new husband wrote about the law as it related to marriage:

> "*Married, she becomes his property, and may become his victim, his slave. She must live where he wishes her to live; she must submit to his embraces, however loathsome; she must bear his children, whether she wish to do so, or not; her property, her liberty, her comfort, her person, her life are all in his power. He will probably be punished for an outright murder by poison or steel, but there are many ways of killing, which she has no power to resist. The subject of his caprices, the victim of his lusts, starved in her sympathies…this human being has but one duty, and that is obedience.*"[46]

Marriage and divorce relate to one common condition: the fallibility of humanity. There would be no need for marriage if people kept their promises without the need for prompting or reminding. Marriage is about the binding of two people, because without the binding there is little security. As such, we realise that marriage is founded on our imperfections, and divorce is recognition that the institution, despite its strengths and values, cannot isolate us from those same imperfections.

Over the decades, attempts to make divorce easier have been opposed by conservatives on the grounds that they weaken marriage. But they don't weaken marriage; they make the institution stronger, because those who seek to marry can be confident there will be justice if a marriage fails.

Marriage and Australia

Australians have always taken marriage laws seriously. Possibly, this is the result of the United Kingdom's marriage law passed in 1753. The law (among other things) required ministers of religion to keep proper marriage records and banned the consecration of private marriages. The penalty for breaching the marriage law was penal servitude in the colonies!

Since 1788, governments have sought to tightly control marriage. At different times, authorities have argued that convicts, Aboriginals, immigrants and people of different races should not have access to marriage. In the words of Rodney Croome, *"We have seen that the history of freedom to marry in Australia is the history of flawed plans to manipulate society by controlling who ordinary people wed, of the defiance of these plans by those who would make this choice themselves, and of the evolution of Australian society this defiance sparked."*[47]

Almost 230 years of Australian history tells us that government interventions in marriage laws have eventually always been found to be wanting. Government has interfered in marriage because it thinks it knows best. However, the best intentions have created a litany of social disasters.

Marriage and Convicts

The question of who should be allowed to marry was a powerful consideration for the authorities in the early days of the colony. Twenty per cent of the convicts who travelled to Australia as part of the First Fleet were female.

During the long voyage, one female convict, Mary Broad, fell pregnant. Two weeks after the arrival of the First Fleet at Port

Jackson, Mary married William Bryant. It was the first marriage in the new settlement.[48]

However, there was no right to marry if you were not a free man or woman. Indeed, having to ask for permission to marry was proof that you did not control the most intimate relationship in your life.

From 1788 to 1868, 162,000 men and women were transported to Australia as convicts.[49] If convicts wanted to marry, they had to apply for permission. However, the decisions that were handed down were arbitrary. Some convicts were encouraged to marry, whilst others were banned from marrying. Members of the clergy sometimes found themselves advocating to the authorities on behalf of couples denied permission to marry.

The system oscillated from generosity to meanness. Pregnancy was not considered a legitimate reason to marry (otherwise authority would have been circumvented by deliberate pregnancies), nor was religious conviction or romantic love considered a valid reason.

For female convicts, marriage meant freedom. Female convicts made pragmatic choices, with some choosing to marry a man they did not love rather than remain a convict. There was incentive for the colony to encourage women to marry, in that the colony was no longer responsible for the female convict once she was married. She was now the responsibility of the husband.

Eventually, successive governors realised that marriage was a means of turning convicts into responsible citizens. It was a way in which convicts could take responsibility for their own lives and for the life of another.

Encouraging convicts to marry was a critical part of the way in which we turned our convict settlements into a free and open society.

Marriage and Aboriginals

If there is shame in the Australian story, it is because of the way we treated our nation's first inhabitants. From the first days of European settlement, the Indigenous people of our country were turned into outsiders in the land that had always been theirs.

Justice was capricious in the young colony, and the new settlers were in no doubt about their superiority to the original inhabitants. This was demonstrated by the various marriage laws.

In the 1880s, Victoria introduced an Aboriginal Protection Act that included provisions regarding who Aboriginals could and could not marry. By the 1930s, similar acts had been passed in Western Australia, the Northern Territory and Queensland. In Queensland, the Act was used to prevent white/black marriages. Western Australia used its Act to stop 'half castes' from marrying other Aborigines. The goal was a horrifying attempt to *"breed out the colour"*. Those who supported such legislation argued that it was an important means of protecting children, as the children of mixed races were said to suffer because of this aberration from God's plan (yes, some arguments never change).

In a world that had become fixated on race and the *'purity of races'*, Australia's race and marriage laws were being compared to those of Europe and the United States.

By stopping Aboriginals from marrying the person they loved, the government forced them to leave their homes and travel to where they could legally settle. Families were upended, and when unmarried women had children, they were often taken from them. They were denied the opportunity to make the most fundamental personal decisions; who they loved and who they would marry.

In 1935, the *'half-caste'* women of Broome signed a petition that was presented to the Western Australian Parliament. The petition included an elegant and gracious argument for the freedom to marry.

They petitioned, *"Sometimes we have the chance to marry a man of our choice. We ask for our Freedom so that when the chance comes along we can rule our lives and make ourselves true and good citizens."*[50]

The women of Broome understood what is at the heart of all human rights, and that is, a right is not an end in itself. A right provided by law is there to assist in the fulfilment of an obligation. In this case, the freedom to marry is the freedom to become better citizens.

In 1938, on the 150th anniversary of white settlement, a national conference proposed a *Ten Point Plan for Aboriginal People*. One of the ten points was the right to marry, *"We recommend that Aborigines and Halfcastes should come under the same marriage laws as white people, and should be free to marry partners of their choice, irrespective of colour."*

It would take another two decades for the calls for an end to racial discrimination in marriage to be heeded. In 1959, the Menzies Government introduced the national Marriage Act, and marriage bans on the basis of race were finally removed across every Australian jurisdiction.

Marriage and immigrants

From the mid-19th century to the mid-20th century, Australia expressed a policy preference for white people over every other race. The 'White Australia' Policy sought to preserve Australia's racial identity as European.

In the words of Prime Minister John Curtin, following the commencement of war with Japan, *"this country shall remain forever the home of the descendants of those people who came here in peace in order to establish in the South Seas an outpost of the British race."*[51]

However, the horrors of the Second World War exposed the dangers and futility of race based policies. Hundreds of thousands of Australian men returned to post-war Australia fully aware of what they had fought for and it was not 'racial purity'.

Some of those Australian servicemen, while stationed in Japan following the Japanese surrender, fell in love with Japanese women. However, the Australian government would not sanction their marriage or allow them to return with Japanese wives. That meant that the soldiers, who had risked all for their country, were forced to marry at the Canadian Embassy and migrate to Canada to start a new life with their brides.

The 'great man' thesis may no longer take centre stage in history textbooks, but the tide of history is still sometimes altered by a single life, and that was the case with Annie Mays Jacob.

In 1942, Annie Mays, along with her husband Samuel and their seven children, sought refuge in Australia as the Japanese advanced through Indonesia. The Jacob family was part of an intake of 15,000 wartime refugees, which included 10,000 people from Nazi-dominated Europe and 5,000 who had escaped the Japanese advance.

After settling in Australia, Annie Mays gave birth to her eighth child and Samuel returned to the Pacific theatre to fight the Japanese. During the course of the conflict, Samuel was killed, and Annie subsequently married her John O'Keith, her landlord. O'Keith had promised Samuel that he would look after Annie Mays and the children if anything happened to Samuel and he kept his promise.

In 1949, the Chifley Government sought to return the Asian refugees who had received asylum in Australia, and the order was given to deport Annie Mays and her children. The order was condemned by her local parish priest and the case was taken up by Archbishop Daniel Mannix.

Eventually, the matter reached the High Court which engaged in judicial hair-splitting to overturn the Government's decision by four votes to two. The Labor Government's Immigration Minister Arthur Calwell flew into a rage, declaring that *"We can have a white Australia, we can have a black Australia, but a mongrel Australia is impossible, and I shall not take the first steps to establish the precedents which will allow the floodgates to be opened."*[52] Tell us what you really think, Arthur!

Calwell promised legislation to overturn the High Court judgment. However, later that year, the Menzies Government was elected to office and the new Immigration Minister, Harold Holt agreed to let all of the Asian refugees stay.

Today we take the link between marriage and citizenship for granted. Provided that the relationship is proved to be genuine and is not a 'sham marriage', people who marry Australians can become citizens.

Marriage and the shift below the surface

The evolution of marriage over the centuries has made it stronger. It is not an anachronism that exists in isolation from the society that it reflects.

Over the past century and a half, we have witnessed an evolution in the belief that underpins marriage. There was a time when marriage was about securing the economic future of individuals and was a licence for procreation. This was a reflection of the times when the family was the only safety net and children were an insurance policy against an impoverished old age. The family was the only thing that protected you from impoverishment. The ABS figures comparing the wealth, income and security of elderly single Australians to those of married couples demonstrates that there is still an economic imperative to marry.

Although marriage provides a safety net, the strength of marriage rests on something deeper, and that is, for most people, that life is easier to navigate with a partner than going it alone.

Marriage now rests on the belief that we marry the person we love, because a lifelong relationship of mutual support and care is the best foundation for an emotionally fulfilling and stable life.

This is a foundation that is based on a commitment to care for another. It reflects a culture of responsibility and a recognition that a rich inner life comes from sharing our life with others. If this is the foundation, then there is no reason why we should deny gay and lesbian people the opportunity to benefit from this institution.

Allowing gays and lesbians to share in the benefits of marriage will not weaken marriage. Instead, it will strengthen marriage and strengthen families and communities. By seeking to marry, gays and lesbians are seeking to build stronger, more committed, lifelong relationships, and to do so with the blessing of their family, friends and the country they love. Gays and lesbians do not seek to change the institution of marriage, but to join it.

Over the past 150 years, humanity has witnessed the greatest changes since the dawn of time. The great strides made in technology, telecommunications, science, medicine and transportation have transformed our existence. Through it all, the institution of marriage has grown stronger. It continues to strengthen couples, undergird families and enrich our national life. It has grown because it has leant into the times. The predicted end of marriage has not eventuated. Had marriage remained frozen in time, stuck in an era where women did not have equal rights, where blacks and whites were not meant to share the same bus seat, let alone the same bed, and where blind obedience triumphed over an individual's aspiration, it would not have become the aspiration it is today.

Those who support same-sex marriage are seeking to make marriage stronger and allow all Australians the opportunity to benefit from it.

Marriage and its legitimacy

As a supporter of same-sex marriage, I winced when former Wallabies captain David Pocock said that he would not marry his fiancée Emma until Australia's marriage laws were changed.

His argument was that he and Emma did not want to participate in a legal ceremony if the same ceremony was not also open to gays and lesbians.

I winced at his comments because, although well intentioned, they diminished a great institution.

Pocock's argument seeks to make every marriage political. His argument is that because same-sex marriage is not legal, then no marriage is legitimate. My premise is that every relationship is legitimate and that's why we must give them all the blessing and support of our civil society.

Pocock's actions demonstrate that without change, marriage will enter the political arena.

However, it need not, and it should not, become political. Marriage should be known for what it celebrates and affirms. As *The Economist* put it over 20 years ago, "*If marriage is to fulfil its aspirations, it must be defined by the commitment of one to another for richer for poorer, in sickness and in health – not by the people it excludes.*"[53]

The Times of London made a similar point in a 2012 editorial: "*Far from damaging marriage, expanding it to same sex couples shores it up... Stable gay relationships are a part of national life. If marital law cannot accommodate them, the purpose of marriage will be brought into question. Gay marriage will be a notable but still evolutionary social reform. And the marriage contract has changed historically to take account of shifting mores.*"⁵⁴

If marriage does not change, it will be drawn deeper into the culture wars, and that would be a pity. The best way for marriage to stay strong is for it to grapple with the changes that are occurring in our societies, and to welcome gay and lesbian people into the ranks of those who marry.

Marriage and the changing face of Australia

It is not only marriage that has changed in Australia; it is our families as well.

In a generation, cohabitation before marriage has become the norm. In 2014, 79 per cent of all couples who married lived together before marriage. This compares with 56 per cent in 1995 and 16 per cent in 1975.⁵⁵

We are also witnessing the rise of single-person households, which now comprise one in four Australian households. This compares with 8 per cent just after the Second World War.

The family, in its various forms, still dominates, our social landscape. There are 6.7 million families in Australia, including 3.9 million families with children (both dependent and non-dependent).⁵⁶

Almost one in two couples (48 per cent) do not have children, although some, of course, will go on to have children.

In families with children aged 17 or under, 74 per cent have two parents, 19 per cent are single-parent families and 6 per cent are step and blended families.

One in five Australian children has a parent who is not living in their family home. In other words, just over 1 million children live in homes where their mum or dad is not living with them. In 87 per cent of single-parent homes, the children live with their mother.

Despite the tremendous change occurring in families, the marriage rate is stable and the divorce rate is falling. In 2012, a record 123,000 couples tied the knot. The 'crude marriage rate' of 5.4 marriages per 1,000 population was comparable to the crude marriage rate of 5.3 in 2003.[57]

As well, the divorce rate is falling. In 2012, 49,900 couples divorced. This equates to 2.1 divorces per 1,000 population and it compares to a rate of 2.7 divorces per 1,000 population in 1993.

We see that despite the changes in attitudes towards cohabitation, sex, and children; marriage remains strong.

Marriage and conservatives

Conservatives look to the past for guidance and a study of the past shows that marriage has changed, and in so doing, has strengthened the social fabric.

This fabric is not ethereal. It is the sum of our human relationships. For over half the population, marriage is an anchor for our lives. It is also an anchor that supports others, for marriage is an invitation to accept responsibility. It allows us to answer the questions: who am I responsible for? Who will I care for when they are sick, or lose their job or feel overwhelmed by the storms of life?

This invitation to accept responsibility is a reflection of the conservative view of life. No one can be compelled to get married, nor can anyone say they have a right to get married (after all, how can we say we have a right to marriage when marriage involves the consent of another?), but it is an opportunity to take responsibility. Marriage is a responsibility to care for another, to support an extended family, to contribute to community and society.

If changes to marriage are consistent with the values of marriage, namely to love, honour and care for another, then these changes will not weaken marriage. In fact, to open marriage up to people who want to uphold its promise will strengthen it.

The winds of change that have moulded marriage over past centuries have not made the institution weaker, but have kept it strong. The institution has leant into the times, changing as it has needed to, like any conservative institution should.

Conservatives should not fear change, although instinctively we are suspicious of it. Rather, we should embrace incremental change as a way of allowing this foundational institution to grow and remain strong.

5

RESPONSIBILITY AND SHAME

"We all suffer periods of illness, sadness, distress, fury. What happens to us, what happens to the people around us, when we desperately need a hand but find none to hold?"
- Jonathan Rauch

The promise of family

When I was a boy and turned in to bed each night, my dad would come in to my room, kneel by my bed and kiss me good night.

Most nights he would say, *"Paul, I love you no matter what. Even if you become a murderer I will still love you!"*

"Daaaaaaadddd," I'd reply, slightly annoyed. *"I'm not going to become a murderer"*.

If we had that conversation once, we had it a thousand times. A murderer, seriously!

It was only as an adult that I realised the point he was making. That no matter what I did in life, no matter my mistakes and errors, my father and mother would still love me.

Straight or gay, lesbian or transgender, single or coupled, everything in life starts with that foundation – the love and acceptance of a family.

Some say that families are founded on emotional bonds. That is true, in part. However, families are also founded on promises. My father's words weren't just meant to reassure me; they were a promise to me.

Love is not just a feeling; it is a promise. Love is proven by action.

Marriage is also a promise. It is the promise of lifelong care: *"to have and to hold from this day forward, for better for worse, for richer for poorer, in sickness and in health, to love, cherish and honour, till death do us part."*

This is not just a promise to a person; it is a promise to family and to society.

Imagine a circumstance where a young man in his early 20s has a terrible accident that means he requires 24-hour care for the rest of his life. He has a girlfriend. They have been dating for six months. After the shock of the accident has passed and the young man has stabilised and returned to his parents' modified family home, his girlfriend makes a decision not to continue the relationship. She says to herself *"It's all too hard. I haven't got the strength to care and support him all my days."*

It is a horrible circumstance, and provided she treats her boyfriend with dignity and respect, most people would be understanding. The relationship is still within her gift. She has made no promise of lifelong care, and because there is no promise, none should be expected.

But what if this couple had been married days before the accident, which occurred on their honeymoon? What if months after the accident she sought a divorce?

Instinctively, we would question her character. She would be walking away from a vow made in front of family and friends to support her husband no matter what. For her to leave him in these circumstances would be a terrible blow to an already wounded person. It would be a betrayal.

Marriage is a promise to care for a person during life's most difficult circumstances. It is a promise that we will not have to endure catastrophe alone.

It is also a promise of support to a couple. Social expectations are the invisible third party in a marriage. The wedding guests are not bystanders. The wedding is a shared memory. It is the day when a family takes a shared stake in a union and its success.

Family and community strengthen us when love, good grace and humour seem to fail us. In marriage, faith, love, tradition, community and the law reinforce each other. This is its power.

Marriage is a conservative ideal. It acknowledges that it is our familial relationships that sustain us in life. They are the tight cords of life's safety net. Conservatives appreciate that families are the foundation to living a life that is not reliant on the state, but interdependent with others.

The former Howard Government minister Amanda Vanstone makes the point that same-sex marriage is a reflection of this ideal:

> "*If you believe as I do you should try and look after yourself, be independent and be an individual, then you are going to have to do that with others. You're going to have to have relationships and admit dependence on other people. That's what people do when they get married. They say 'We are going to be dependent on each other'. I think conservatives should welcome more people openly saying 'I'm going to have a life relationship with this person, we will be dependent on each other, we are going to ask things of each other instead of asking from the State'. I think conservatives should welcome more recognition of interdependence.*"[58]

At the heart of enduring families is the understanding that families are about our shared responsibility.

Indeed, it is often at the time when unexpected events hit that gay and lesbian people find themselves without the legal support they need. It is after the accident, or in the ICU, or when the guardian is needed to sign the form to donate organs, or possibly at the funeral home, that gay and lesbian people have to explain the relationship they have with their partner. The words 'husband' and 'wife' are culturally and legally understood, but the meaning of the word 'partner' is blurred. Are the couple in a long-term relationship or are they casually dating? It is never quite clear.

A wedding vow is a solemn promise that reflects the best of our humanity. No one has argued, nor can they argue, that gay, lesbian, transgender, bisexual and intersex people do not have the same capacity for love, devotion and care as anyone else, or that they are not suited to making lifelong commitments to each other.

All of us benefit from love and attachment, from commitment and loyalty, from the testing that comes from sharing our lives with another.

Most of us have lived through seasons where the costs of our attachments and loyalties seem to exceed the benefits. However, these deficits in our emotional lives are temporary. Mostly, over the span of a life, we benefit more from the deep and lasting interactions we have with the people we love. It is what makes us human, and it is what we should always support and encourage.

Young journalists often write stories about the cost of having children. Yes, children are expensive, and they demand sacrifices. In my own life, I remember my dad working Monday to Friday as a bus driver, and then backing up on the weekend by driving cabs. Mum was a nurse and worked two to four shifts a week in addition to getting us off to school and running a home.

As I have discovered in my own life, raising kids is a glorious privilege. A child is an affirmation of the life we have been given and the hope of what lies ahead. This yearning for our children to have a better life is common to all parents, no matter their age, race or sexuality.

The privilege and responsibility of raising a child is not a one-way street. My parents are in their 70s, and still spritely and totally independent, but old age is slowly creeping in. I hope they have their faculties and independence all their days, but if they don't, then my sisters and I will step in to care for them. That's what families do. Why? Because to deny the people you love is to deny yourself, it is to walk away from the essence of your being.

Our individual achievements mean nothing if we cannot share them with the people we love and our virtue means little if we do not care for our own family when it is in need.

Recently, the mother of one of my friends died following a protracted battle with cancer that lasted for almost five years. During it all, my friend and his partner did what they could to make her days easier – regular visits, phone calls to check on her, a spot of gardening, stayovers to take the pressure off his father, lifts to doctors' appointments, odd jobs and keeping quiet vigil when death drew near.

My friend's partner cared for my friend's mother as though she was his own. By law, he is not part of that family, but by deed and heart, he surely is. Same-sex marriage for that couple would be a legal confirmation of what they already are – responsible people who pledge lifelong devotion to each other and the families of which they are part.

Marriage is the means by which strangers become kin. Families have never been strictly about biology. We all have relatives with whom we do not share the same blood. I can think of uncles, cousins and in-laws with whom I share no DNA, but they share the same place in my heart as those who do. Because they are family, there is a responsibility to support them through life's trials.

Throughout history, family has never been solely about blood. Different cultures and times have defined families according to their circumstances. For the Romans, the family consisted of those who lived under the one roof. In medieval times, it included those with whom you laboured and lived with in the community.

The make-up of the family has also changed. A century ago, raising a dozen children was not unheard of. In part, the birthrate was high because child mortality was high, contraception was unreliable and social expectations were for large families. Since that time, the size of families in Western countries has consistently fallen. In Australia, the female fertility rate is now 1.9 births per woman, compared with 3.5 in the early 1960s.

The 20th century also saw the emergence of adoption, although numbers have fallen substantially in recent years. The legal embrace of adoption recognised that in some cases, parenthood was not a blood relationship, but a psychological and emotional one. The first adoption laws were strongly opposed. Adoption was viewed as 'unnatural', as it was not founded on blood ties (although in some cases parents adopted nieces and nephews). It was, according to its critics, an attack on the family and an attempt to weaken or even dismantle a sacred institution.

Like those who oppose same-sex marriage today, those who opposed adoption failed to see that love, affection, commitment and a willingness to sacrifice are at the core of strong and enduring families. The adopted child, the beneficiary of this grace, had a second chance to grow up in a secure, loving environment.

The most precious things in a family are the deep emotional ties that bind its members. It is the willingness to nurture, love and make sacrifices that defines a family.

Denying people choices never protects the family unit. When you deny people the freedom to marry the person they love, face their own challenges and make their own mistakes, you also deny them the freedom to triumph over them and to prove that love conquers all.

The family is an institution that leans into the times. Every generation hears the cry that the family is under threat, but families are nimble and respond to the times. Throughout history, marriage has evolved in response to economic, social and cultural changes. Instead, of driving change, marriage has traditionally responded to it. As such, change is safer for the institution because it is bringing legal equilibrium to what has already occurred.

The culture of responsibility

One of the central tenets of all religions is that human beings are better than animals. We are more than biology. We have within us the power of reason, the power to choose between right and wrong.

This power is found in responsibility. We are interdependent, and our relationships have meaning. As children, most of us are gently pointed towards a roadmap for life – to devote ourselves to another, establish roots in a community, raise a family and enjoy the fruits of our labour.

We implicitly see the interconnectedness between devoting ourselves to others and having a meaningful life. The foundation of a thriving inner life comes from others. It is built not on rights, but on responsibilities.

In some ways, the case for same-sex marriage has been sabotaged by the focus on 'rights'. The law denies same-sex couples the right to marry, but Australians seek changes to the law as part of a 'roadmap to responsibility' which benefits us all.

Because marriage strengthens society, mutual responsibility strengthens the social fabric and interdependence is the core of every community, the law should support and affirm the most important of human relationships – the person with whom we choose to share our life with.

By preventing same-sex couples from marrying, the law as it currently stands diminishes the sovereignty of some of our citizens to lead responsible lives. John Stuart Mill wrote over two centuries ago that *"the only purpose for which power can be rightfully exercised over any member of a civilised community, against his will, is to prevent harm to others. ... In the part which merely concerns himself, his independence is, of right, absolute. Over himself, over his own body and mind, the individual is sovereign."*[59]

As it stands, the law does not allow some citizens to be sovereign over the most important choice they face as an adult – to legally wed the person with whom they seek to spend the rest of their life. The law should be blind when it comes to the people we love, because this is what the individual should be sovereign over. By allowing gays and lesbians the opportunity to marry the person they love, we allow partners to become spouses.

The term 'partner', in the words of the columnist David Brooks, *"reeks of contingency"*.[60] It implies that we are committed to, but not 100 per cent settled on, the relationship. It might not be permanent. It is a term that is mostly appropriated from business, and it speaks of a relationship that only exists while there is mutual benefit. To be fair, there is also a degree of honesty in the term, and it can speak of the relationship as it currently exists. It is a term used by many couples before they decide to marry.

However, it is a term that many gays and lesbians, by virtue of the law, have been stuck with. A partner is not a legal part of a family, nor is a partner considered a lifelong companion, no matter how long he or she has been by the side of another. No matter the depth of a couple's love for and devotion to each other, the relationship suffers from the tyranny of low expectations rather than being given every chance to reflect life's loftiest ideals.

In putting the case for marriage and its value to families, I do not sugarcoat the fact that many marriages struggle to go the distance.

The columnist Peter FitzSimons recently remarked about his 25-year marriage to TV personality Lisa Wilkinson that in any year *"We have 50 blissful days, 300 pretty good days and 15 shockers. But as we've got older...15 shockers are now down to three."*[61] The longer the marriage, the longer the relationship, the more I suspect people nod their head and in the recesses of their own mind, insert their own numbers into FitzSimons' 365 day equation.

In a way, FitzSimons points to the lifecycle of all marriages, with their ebbs and flows of devotion, the tensions that arise from our failings, and for those fortunate enough, the unexpected emergence of a quiet and steadfast certainty that carries us through good and bad times.

We are all buffeted by life. Mostly, marriage works. Two in three marriages are lifelong, and there is no reason to suggest that the marriage of two men or two women will be any different.

Still, the opponents of same-sex marriage argue that some same-sex marriages will fail – and on this, we agree. Some same-sex marriages will fail, just like some heterosexual marriages will fail. However, that is not a sufficient reason to deny gays and lesbians the opportunity to make their own promises and to keep their own commitments.

Importantly, marriage will add new strength to these relationships. Marriage is a contract witnessed and supported by family and friends, and is an institution supported not just by law, but by social expectations. Our family, friends and loved ones have a vested interest in seeing a marriage succeed.

A wedding is more than a celebration. It is the shared memory of love and support for a couple. It is the communal declaration that the witnesses have a shared stake in this union and its success. This is the invisible glue that sets marriage apart from every other relationship.

When teenagers first date, there is no expectation that it will last. Life has taught us that it is only a matter of time before a young heart is broken. For the teenager, it is painful, but he or she grows from the experience. The teenager is supported by the social expectation that it is okay to break it off when need be, to keep looking and to love again. We see it as a natural part of growing up and finding out about ourselves.

Marriage is different. The hope is that it will succeed. Faith, love, tradition, the law and the community reinforce each other – they form the expectation that the relationship will last.

Same-sex couples are expected to uphold the same standards but the law, as it stands, does not give these couples the same support. There is an irony in this as for decades we have witnessed an expansion in the rights of 'de facto' partnerships. 'De facto' couples have been given the rights of marriage without the responsibilities. This extension of rights has occurred as a matter of justice. It means that fathers and long-term partners are required to support their children and their former partner should they separate.

However, gays and lesbians are not asking for rights without responsibilities; rather, they are asking for rights and responsibilities. This is surely a conservative ideal.

Supporting children

Across Australia, there are about 6,300 children living with same-sex parents. On any weekday morning, the parents and children in these families face the same rush as any other family. The parents are trying to get sleepy kids out of bed and promising themselves that tonight, the kids will go to bed early. Meanwhile, one child can't find his running shoes for the sports carnival and another yells *"We've run out of milk!"* As breakfast is quickly eaten, the children are reminded that *"No electronic devices are to be used at the table"* at the same time as the phone beeps with a message from work. All the while, parents are packing lunches, pressing shirts, making arrangements for after-school activities and trying to get the kids out the door so everyone can get to school and work on time.

For some, these parents and children aren't a real family, because the children's conception wasn't the same as that of most other children. Frankly, for this family, it's been a long time since any parent talked about conception! That's because conception is just a moment in a lifetime, but parenting is for life.

Straight or gay, the foundations for raising healthy, well-adjusted children are the same; an education, a job and two parents staying together.

The focus of family policy should always be: what's good for kids. We know what isn't good for kids – a lifetime on welfare, instability in relationships, family violence, drug and alcohol abuse, community service interventions, parents in correctional facilities and living in unstable communities.

For people interested in family policy, these are the intractable challenges facing some Australian families, and they reflect a deeper reality. There are parts of Australia, particularly remote Australia, where the institutions of community and family are failing. The intractable challenges facing these families are profoundly real, and children are growing up ill-equipped for a job, further studies or stable relationships.

Other than their love, the most important thing a parent can offer their child is stability. In the words of one expert, *"A child can handle almost anything better than instability."*

More children than ever are being raised in single-parent homes.

That is not to lambast single parents. On the contrary, single parents are doing the job of two people, and if anyone needs support it is them. However, as Kevin Andrews has pointed out, in just a generation, we have seen the proportion of single-parent homes double from one in ten to one in five. Two-thirds of these homes rely on welfare to get through the week.

The challenge for our nation is not the make-up of homes; it's the state of some homes. Our families are not strengthened by denying same-sex families the support of the institution of marriage, but they are strengthened by jobs, education and support for parents. In the debates that shape our country, this is where conservatives need to engage.

By virtue of biology, same-sex couples have to seek assistance if they want to have children. Adoption, surrogacy and IVF are expensive processes. Depending on what path is chosen, it can require lawyers, bank loans and great patience. It is not a path that is chosen lightly.

According to the University of Queensland's *Not So Private Lives* study of same-sex attracted people, 35 per cent of partnered lesbians have or are expecting children (this includes a proportion who have children from an earlier heterosexual relationship) and 21 per cent plan on having children (this includes some overlap, as some of those who already have children will want to have more).[62]

Similarly, 14 per cent of partnered gay men are raising children (this includes men who have had children with female partners) and 11 per cent want children.

Based on this data, we can assume that up to half of all lesbian couples and anywhere from 10 to 20 per cent of gay couples either already have or plan on having children.

This is not all that dissimilar to the US Census data, which shows that 20 per cent of male couple households and 23 per cent of female couple households are raising children.

Whether or not same-sex couples are allowed to marry, children will continue to be born to and raised by gay and lesbian parents. However, by denying gays and lesbians the opportunity to marry, we are denying their children and their families the strength that comes from marriage as an institution.

In the same way in which children change heterosexual couples, they change same-sex couples. Like all parents, same-sex parents find that their focus shifts from spending time with friends to spending time with their children. Many same-sex parents find that they have more in common with other parents than with their friends who do not have children. This mirrors the experience of all parents.

Children are a force for good in the lives of gay and lesbian parents, just as they are in the lives of heterosexual parents.

At funerals, it is often remarked how much we owe our parents, and that is true. There is also a quiet truth that parents don't often speak about, and that is how much we owe our children. To be in a front-row seat witnessing a human life unfold and to watch a person emerge into adulthood with all of its joys and challenges is one of life's great privileges.

Children remind us that there is more to life than a career or a bigger home or a promotion. They ground us. The Queen once said that *"grief is the price we pay for love,"*[63] and parenthood has its own grief. As parents, we watch the people we love more than life itself face their own challenges, and all too often we are powerless to help.

In the best way possible, children make us feel alive and reconnect us to the life of our families and to a life beyond possessions and positions. Raising children is a privilege, and gay and lesbian couples are already making sacrifices to raise their children. Some are acting as foster parents, while others are adopting and giving a child the love it so desperately needs. Other couples, like infertile heterosexual couples are using IVF, artificial insemination and surrogacy.

There are some people who are instinctively or morally opposed to any form of medical assistance to help infertile heterosexual couples and same-sex couples have children. I respect that. However, questions about how a child is conceived do not negate our responsibility to help these children grow up to become strong, responsible citizens.

The best thing we can do for these children is to support the foundational relationships in their lives – and that means supporting their parents. Children need stable homes, and marriage is the glue that helps hold many families together.

Answering the wounds of shame

Walking into the Prime Minister's suite of offices after a change of government should be an exhilarating moment, but for me it wasn't. It was the moment when my 'mid-life crisis' truly hit.

It had been brewing for some time, but being the strong, silent type, I was able to hide it from everyone except Sarah and the girls.

My strategy to escape my gnawing anxiety was to work harder than ever. At work, I was determined to work longer than anyone else. The days started with 6am conference calls and I was still at my desk late at night, every night. Throwing myself into my job felt like a relief from the pressure I was feeling when I was alone.

At home, I was irritable. I was snapping when I shouldn't have, and wasn't wholly present when I should have been. At one level, the stress was easy to explain. We'd moved house, moved cities, set the kids up in new schools and I was in a frenetic job with a BlackBerry that never seemed to stop beeping.

But there was this knot in my stomach that continued to grow as the election drew closer and closer. A lifetime of doubts grew to a crescendo.

My inner and outer worlds seemed fundamentally disconnected. In my outer world, I was a husband and father of two, an author, had three degrees including one from Harvard, had won professional awards for my work and was Senior Adviser to the Prime Minister. Yet in my inner world, I felt like a failure, not living up to my own hopes or the expectations of others and the demands of my faith.

Of course, it seemed entirely irrational to be working in an office only a few feet from the centre of power and to feel like I did.

It was a few months into government that I stumbled across a book by Brene Brown entitled *I Thought It Was Just Me (But It Isn't)*. It found me at just the right time and most mornings after my 6am call with the Prime Minister, I took myself off to a coffee shop and I read and re-read Brown as though it was a sacred text. I started journaling again, and in putting pen to paper, drew out my hopes and disappointments, my frustrations as well as fears. I talked to close friends, and asked myself about the foundations of my life.

All in all, I started to reflect deeply on the issue of shame in my life, and more broadly about my life, my family, my faith and what it means to participate in politics during a time when it is more brutal than ever. In some ways, this book is a continuation of that reflection, an attempt to answer the question of how can we accept people for who they are and sit comfortably with our differences.

Shame is that sense of not being good enough, not having enough and not fitting in enough. It can result from the wrinkles on our face, the income we earn, the job we hold, the stammer that plagues us, the marriage that failed, the weight we can't lose, the job we lost because of our drinking, the children we have failed or the sexual abuse that we suffered as a child.

All too often, we project our shame onto others, quietly saying to ourselves *"compared to them, I am better"*.

We tell ourselves that the negative self-talk is good for us and that no one is tougher on us than ourselves. But if that were true, we'd all be a perfect weight, we wouldn't smoke or battle addictions and we'd look like the people on TV. Instead, our journeys are gritty and imperfect, and we need others more than we'd care to admit.

As social beings, we value the opinions of others, but it doesn't matter what others think, they will think what they will. What matters is, have I been true to what I believe?

Shame does not stand alone. It is always accompanied by fear, blame and disconnection and we try to shake off the feelings of being diminished, ignored, ridiculed, flawed or unworthy.

So why is this relevant to a book on same-sex marriage?

Because it's what our society has loaded on gay, lesbian, bisexual, transgender and intersex people since the arrival of the First Fleet. We've said *"Compared with them, I am better"*.

We criminalised gay Australians, even those who were willing to risk their lives for their country.

We let discrimination flourish, and turned a blind eye to violence and humiliation.

We mocked and laughed, and let it be known that gays and lesbians were not part of us.

And at all times, we demanded their silence. We said, you can do what you want in your bedrooms, but we don't want to know about it. We don't want to know about you.

Worst of all, we said, through word and deed, that gays and lesbians were incapable of love. Some are still saying that today.

I attended an all-boys' school. It was for me a good school, and I have happy memories of it. However, I remember two Year 12 students who were a year ahead of me. They were good friends to each other, but to everyone else they were 'poofs'. Were they gay? I don't know, and it doesn't matter.

As far as I can recall, I never spoke to them and never taunted them, but that didn't mean I didn't know their names. We all did. One day in the middle of term, they were gone. No goodbyes. No farewells. Nothing. The taunting finally broke them.

If we are honest, we all have a story like that — because that was Australia for far too long.

By criminalising homosexuality, we made it an object of shame. The shame of communities was brought into families. The son or daughter who was the apple of their father's or mother's eye became tarnished. In some families, there was 'don't ask, don't tell' whereby sons and daughters hid their lives and their loves from the family they loved. But if you are not truly accepted, you can't truly belong, and in some way, all our families were diminished.

Some say we cannot fully understand sexism, racism, homophobia, ageism and other forms of judgment unless we have experienced them. That might be true, but at some point we have all experienced the real or imagined judgment of others. It is experienced in comments about our bodies, our parenting, our families, our finances, our work, our age, our health and our sex.

One of the compelling reasons why same-sex marriage is important for the gay, lesbian, bisexual, transgender and intersex people of Australia is that nothing speaks of acceptance more than marriage.

It is so much more than a piece of paper. It is the joyful celebration of two complete lives made for each other.

Marriage allows gay and lesbian teenagers to have the same hopes for love, family and life as their straight brothers and sisters.

Acceptance is a powerful force for good. It is an antidote to fear.

Speechwriters are mostly discreet about the speeches they help write, because it's not their speech, it's the speech of the person they write for. Ted Sorensen, the famous speechwriter to President Kennedy, was asked at an event I attended: *"Did you write the words – 'Ask not what your country can do for you, ask what you can do for your country'?"* Sorensen replied, *"Ask not."*

I generally subscribe to the Sorensen view of speeches in relation to the words I crafted as the Prime Minister's speechwriter. However, there was one set of remarks that touched me deeply which I want to share. During 2015, Tony Abbott was asked to introduce the *Australian Story* profile of his transgender friend Cate McGregor.

Australian Story always has an element of mystery in its introduction and the producers of the programme did not want the Prime Minister alluding to the centrepiece of the story, the gender transition of Malcolm to Cate.

I told the producers no. I never wanted anyone to think that Tony Abbott would not mention Cate's transition in her gender. I didn't want it said that the Prime Minister was embarrassed by having a transgender friend, because he wasn't. The Prime Minister would only participate if he had the opportunity to speak about Cate's life. Eventually, we reached an agreement with the Prime Minister opening the programme and also closing it.

Prior to filming, I gave the Prime Minister his draft remarks, and with his trademark illegible scribbles, he made just a few changes. I can't say the words were mine, because a good speechwriter is always trying to anticipate what their principal would and should say. As well, Tony Abbott was already on the record about his admiration of Cate McGregor. Even if it was my draft, the words were his sentiments.

This is what Tony Abbott said:

"Cate and I met in student days and we've been friends through all the

ups and downs of our lives for almost 30 years. She's an author, an army officer and my guru in all things cricket. Most recently she helped me to put together the team for my inaugural Prime Minister's XI match. Cate's love for cricket has been a constant throughout.

As you watch her story tonight, I know you will see the friend I know — a person of strength, intellect, capacity and truly remarkable courage."

At the end of the programme, he concluded:

"As well as Cate's passion for cricket, there's been another constant in her life and that's been a wrenching struggle over identity. It took remarkable courage to acknowledge this and even more to make such a massive change in her life.

Her name has changed but her character and soul have not. I am very proud to call Cate my friend."

Even now, I can hear the voice of Tony Abbott saying *"Her name has changed but her character and soul have not."*

The night the programme went to air, I was working back again. I loved the quietness of the PMO in the evening; it was like being in a warm cocoon. As a writer, the evenings were some of my most productive times, and often by 9pm I'd be wandering the office looking for someone to whom I could read the latest draft of a speech. I was curious about how the *Australian Story* remarks had been received, and so I went online and came across two transgender people discussing what the programme meant to them.

One said to the other about Tony Abbott's comments, *"This is our Redfern speech."*

It was the last thing in the world I expected to read. To my amazement, I started to cry. When I think of that moment, I still do.

As a speechwriter, there was no finer compliment, and as a man, I saw the way in which the words I'd helped write had made a difference. If some outsiders to our national life were made to feel that they were part of our national story, then it was all worth it.

I am not transgender. I cannot imagine the pain and suffering of living your life in a body that is at odds with your sex. To be frank, I don't understand it, nor can I explain it. However, that doesn't mean I cannot offer a hand of acceptance to help make a transgender person's life easier.

Our national story should be one where everyone feels a part, where we can all make a contribution and where no should feel ashamed of who they are, or what they believe.

Allowing same-sex marriage is not just about ensuring that gay and lesbian people feel more at home in their families, communities and national life; it's also about all of us sharing in a country where we all feel accepted for who we are.

6

RENDER UNTO CAESAR

"Is it lawful to pay a poll-tax to Caesar, or not? Shall we pay or shall we not pay?"
But Jesus, knowing their hypocrisy, said to them, "Why are you testing me? Bring me a denarius to look at." They brought one.
And He said to them, "Whose likeness and inscription is this?"
And they said, "Caesar's."
Jesus said to them, "Render to Caesar the things that are Caesar's, and to God the things that are God's."
- Matthew 12: 14 - 17

At the crux of the debate on same-sex marriage is the question, – Is marriage a 'holy secular institution' or a 'wholly secular institution', or is it possibly both?

Some, like Cardinal George Pell, argue that the institution is divine in nature and is owned by religious organisations. In his words, *"Marriage is pre-political and the state has inherited marriage. The state should not alter and supply different reasons for an institution which it has inherited."*[64]

Cardinal Pell is partly right and partly wrong. The church does predate the state in its involvement in the registration of marriage, but only by a century or so.

The church made marriage a sacrament in the 12th century, and by the 15th century church blessings and registration of weddings were the accepted form of registration for marriages.

In the 16th century, the English and French governments legislated for the state to register weddings. Both the church and the state have a claim to modern marriage because it is a hybrid of history.

Tensions in the historical, secular and religious dimensions of marriage are not new. Lord Stowell wrote in an 1811 judgment of the Consistory Court of London:

> *"Marriage, in its origin, is a contract of natural law; it may exist between two individuals of different sexes, although no third person existed in the world, as happened in the case of the common ancestors of mankind. It is the parent, not the child, of civil society... In civil society it becomes a civil contract, regulated and prescribed by law, and endowed with civil consequences. In most civilized countries acting under a sense of the force of sacred obligations, it has had the sanctions of religion superadded. It then becomes a religious, as well as a natural and civil contract; for it is a great mistake to suppose that, because it is the one, therefore it may not likewise be the other."*

In Australia, civil marriage and church marriage sit side by side. Couples have the choice of a marriage conducted according to the rites of their faith, or a civil marriage where aspects of the ceremony and vows can be individualised according to the desires of the couple. Both are recognised by the same law.

For couples having their union solemnised before a non-religious marriage celebrant, the only legally required words to be spoken by the bride and groom are, "*I call upon the persons here present to witness that I, (insert name), take thee, (insert name), to be my lawful wedded wife/husband.*"

All celebrants, religious and otherwise, are required to state the legal meaning of marriage: *"Marriage, according to law in Australia, is the union of a man and a woman to the exclusion of all others, voluntarily entered into for life."* This provision was introduced by the Howard Government in 2004 when it sought to head off a court challenge to the *Marriage Act*.

According to the law, only marriage celebrants registered by the

Commonwealth are allowed to perform marriages. The only legal requirement on celebrants is that they must be of good standing in the community.

As at 2011, there were over 34,000 marriage celebrants in Australia, including 23,500 ministers of religion, 10,200 civil celebrants and 500 authorised registry officers. While civil celebrants account for only 30 per cent of celebrants, they perform 74 per cent of ceremonies.[65]

The influence of religious institutions on marriage has been waning for at least two generations. Half a century ago, almost all weddings were church services. By 1999, civil marriages had overtaken religious marriages for the first time, and the gap has steadily widened since then.

Most of the weddings I have attended (including my own) have been church weddings. That is a product of the influence of the Christian church on my family and friends. Church weddings are the most familiar to me. However, Australians are increasingly choosing non-religious services for their weddings. For most Australians, marriage is no longer the gift of the Church. It is a legal right, and one that most argue should be extended.

Protection for religions and religious celebrants

While religious practice has fallen over the past half century, Australians overwhelmingly believe in the rights of religious institutions to practice the rites of their faith.

Surveys have shown that Australians do not want to force churches to conduct weddings against the tenets of their faith. In 2012, the Senate conducted an inquiry into two bills calling for same-sex marriage to be legalised. To assist the inquiry, the Senate invited

Australians to make a submission and participate in a survey on same-sex marriage. Over 276,000 people participated in the survey. Of those surveyed, 177,000 people (64 per cent) indicated that they were in support of same-sex marriage while 98,000 (36 per cent) were against it. However, when asked if they believed that "*Authorised celebrants, being ministers of religion, should not be obligated to perform same-sex marriages*" a resounding 214,000 people (85 per cent) agreed, and 37,000 people (15 per cent) disagreed.[66]

What is particularly significant about this result is that it was not based on a representative sample of Australians. Instead, the survey attracted people who had a deep interest in the issue of same-sex marriage. The survey showed that even among the most dedicated supporters of same-sex marriage, an overwhelming number did not believe that religious celebrants should be compelled to perform same-sex marriages.

This has been a consistent view of advocates for same-sex marriage. As the Massachusetts Supreme Court noted in its landmark judgment on same-sex marriage, "*Our decision in no way limits the rights of individuals to refuse to marry persons of the same sex for religious or any other reasons. It in no way limits the personal freedom to disapprove of, or to encourage others to disapprove of, same-sex marriage.*"[67]

In Australia, citizens have protection from government-prescribed religion, and religions have protection from the excesses of the state. In the words of former High Court Justice Michael Kirby, "*It is the principle of secularism that protects everyone of any religion, or of no religion.*"[68] A religious group or society is best protected by a secular state and a secular state does not impose restrictions on religion.

The Marriage Act already provides protections for religious freedom. Section 47 of the Act states that nothing in the Act relating to the solemnisation of marriage:

"(a) imposes an obligation on an authorised celebrant, being a minister of religion, to solemnise any marriage; or
(b) prevents such an authorised celebrant from making it a condition of his or her solemnising a marriage that:
(i) longer notice of intention to marry than that required by this Act is given;
(ii) or requirements additional to those provided by this Act are observed."

Section 45 (1) of the Act also states:

"Where a marriage is solemnised by or in the presence of an authorised celebrant, being a minister of religion, it may be solemnised according to any form and ceremony recognised as sufficient for the purpose by the religious body or organisation of which he or she is a minister."

Not one of the bills put before Parliament has sought to change sections 45 or 47 of the Marriage Act. Frankly, to do so would incite every church in the country to campaign against any elected representative who voted for it.

To remove the intent of sections 45 and 47 would also expose the Commonwealth to a High Court challenge based on section 116 of the Constitution.

The Australian Constitution has strong protection for freedom of religion. Section 116, entitled, *"Commonwealth not to legislate in respect of religion"*, states:

"The Commonwealth shall not make any law for establishing any religion, or for imposing any religious observance, or for prohibiting the free exercise of any religion, and no religious test shall be required as a qualification for any office or public trust under the Commonwealth."

If attempts were made to force religions to marry people against their faith, the various religions would no doubt take the matter to the High Court. They would argue that forcing clerics to perform marriages against the doctrines of their faith amounts to *"prohibiting the free exercise of their religion*" as well as imposing a "*religious observance*" on them.

This is a strong legal protection. Public opinion may change, and Acts of Parliament may change, but it is extremely difficult for the Constitution to change.

Since Federation, there have been 44 referenda to change the Constitution, of which only eight have been successful. Of those eight successful referenda, six were not contentious (achieving 'yes' votes of between 70 and 90 per cent). In more than 115 years of our Federation, only two referenda have been passed that were the result of contested debate.

Can I imagine any possibility of the Australian people voting to remove their protection to worship as they see fit and not have a state religion imposed on them? Not in a thousand years.

What if the majority was a minority?

While it is impossible to foresee any changes in our lifetime that would engender a dramatic turn in public opinion, let us consider this idea for just a few minutes.

Let us imagine what would happen if public opinion changed, and the Marriage Act and the Constitution were amended so that churches were required by law to solemnise same-sex marriages.

The straight-forward outcome is that any Act requiring religions to marry same-sex couples against their beliefs would result in them cancelling their celebrants' licences en masse. In turn, it could be expected that religious couples would refuse to accept the authority of the state over their personal lives and decline the option of a civil marriage. The churches would return to doing what they did before the advent of civil marriages – offering a religious sacrament or a blessing for couples.

In other words, the couple would be married in the eyes of the church but not in the eyes of the law. Naturally, family law provisions would protect the couple and their children, and their relationship would be recognised within families. But the relationship would not have the imprimatur of the state or the sanction of the broader community. It would become more ambiguous. The couple would say they were married, but would they really be married?

In other words, what religious groups fear is that religious couples will be treated in the same way as same-sex relationships are treated today.

If we walk a mile in another's shoes, we see life through their eyes.

If people of faith are offended by the possibility of government regulating the practice of their faith and a sacrament of the church, is it not akin to the isolation gays and lesbians feel as a result of the state refusing to accept the legitimacy of their primary relationship?

Governments should treat all people equally, and should not elevate one community over another. In *A Jurisprudence Coming Out: Religion, Homosexuality, and Collisions of Liberty and Equity in American Public Law*, Yale Professor of Law, William Eskridge makes the point that *"The state must allow individual nomic communities to flourish or wither as they may, and the state cannot as a normal matter become the means for the triumph of one community over all others."*

Marriage is a civil and religious institution, and it cannot be disentangled without doing damage to both. Both have their place – the religious wedding for people of faith and the civil wedding for those who feel more at home in a civil setting.

The proponents of same-sex marriage are not seeking to change religious marriage and thereby interrupt the free practice of religion. Instead, the proponents of same-sex marriage are seeking to change civil marriage and to avail themselves of their full rights as free men and women.

The place of conscience

For the first year and a half of the Abbott Prime Ministership, I was the sole speechwriter in the Prime Minister's Office.

The Department had a small speech-writing unit, with fine writers and professional staff, but it was not allowed to send political or partisan speeches to the Prime Minister's office. While we often tried to get the speechwriters in front of the boss, it didn't happen as much as I would have liked, and so at times the speechwriters struggled to capture his voice.

Every day, I was "Abbott-ising" the Department's speeches, writing the speeches they were not allowed to write, managing our social media posts, providing direction over the correspondence and email system and being loaded up with the difficult writing tasks that others didn't want to do. I was working 14 hour days, but still did not have time to work on longer-term issues.

I needed a second speechwriter. Throughout my time in the PMO, I intermittently had contact with a young policy analyst in the Department named Jason Deutsch. Jason was just 28 years of age but wrote with a depth way beyond his years. He was a quiet man and a powerful and beautiful writer who wrote from the soul.

In early 2015, I offered Jason the role of Speechwriter to the Prime Minister. I expected him to immediately accept, as for him, it was a big career break.

Jason said he would accept the job on one condition. This surprised me, because most people don't risk a job in the PMO. Jason's condition was that he wouldn't write a speech that violated his conscience, and that included writing anything in opposition to same-sex marriage.

I agreed to his request because it was proof that his writing reflected a deep integrity. Like mine, his writing came from deep within.

I also had a deep affinity with his position. Jason's realisation that he could not write a speech against same-sex marriage reflected my own wrestling with the same issue.

During his time as Prime Minister, Tony Abbott had never given a prepared speech on same-sex marriage, but I dreaded the day when I would be asked to write such a speech. The closest he had come to anything beyond a simple restating of his view was when he was asked a question by Bill Shorten in May 2015 and responded *"If our Parliament were to make a big decision on a matter such as this, it ought to be owned by the Parliament"*. At the time, Warren Entsch and others were advocating for a conscience vote and I felt the temperature rising on the issue.

If the matter was to come before the Parliament, I had to work on the assumption that the Prime Minister would speak in opposition to the matter, and I would have to draft his remarks.

At a personal level, I felt conflicted. To be the speechwriter to a prime minister is a unique privilege. The prime minister's speechwriter, along with the chief of staff, press secretary, national security adviser, and chief economist is one of the few roles that set the direction of a prime minister's office. It is one of the few jobs where you work one-on-one with the Prime Minister on a daily basis.

However, I dreaded writing a speech that I did not believe in. I felt the country was ready to give gays and lesbians the opportunities for a better life that came from opening up marriage.

To be fair to Tony Abbott, I never raised my internal struggles with him. As we moved closer to a debate on the issue, it weighed heavily on my conscience. I thought about talking with him, but given that the issue was still a 'hypothetical' and there were a lot of bigger issues happening across the government, I felt like it was the last thing in the world I should raise.

Having known Tony for a quarter of a century, I knew he would never ask me to do something I felt uncomfortable with. It was the decency of the man that made me struggle with this issue. I didn't want to let him down, because he had always been so good to me. He had always given me the loyalty for which he was known. I have never had a more supportive or encouraging boss.

However, the events of September 2015 intervened, and I was not asked to write the speech. What might have happened in the world of hypotheticals? I can only guess what might have happened if I was asked to write that speech. I suspect I would have written it but also found a way to express my personal views to the Prime Minister. I would have sought to reconcile my conscience with the responsibilities of my job.

Why would I have considered writing a speech given my internal struggles with it? Because, from my perspective, there would still have been an opportunity to do good through my work. I could have written the speech using language that affirmed gay and lesbian Australians and renounced any arguments or language from others that did not. I could have fashioned remarks that set the limits of the debate as well as state the Prime Minister's preparedness to accept the will of the Parliament.

Of course, in my internal world I would have been walking a tightrope – writing a speech for the 'no case' while silently supporting the 'yes case' would not have sat easily with me.

While I was never asked to write that speech, it gave me a deep appreciation of those who struggle with their conscience on this issue. For those who might applaud Jason's decision and understand my struggle, I ask, would you give the same support to a speechwriter for Bill Shorten, Tanya Plibersek or Anthony Albanese who couldn't write their speeches because of a personal religious belief?

If we believe in the rights of people to exercise their conscience, then they must apply to all. We must respect the conscience of people on both sides of this debate.

Consciences matter. They matter in the Prime Minister's Office and they matter in every other part of Australian life. It is not an easy thing to wrestle with conscience and to find ways of trying to reconcile different beliefs and expectations.

We should not expect people to violate their conscience, because in violating your conscience you violate yourself.

In this debate, two freedoms intersect – the right of religious people to practice their faith and to express that faith, as well as the right of other citizens to live out their lives free of discrimination and prejudice.

How we legally and socially reconcile these conflicting freedoms is the question eloquently asked by *The Australian*'s Editor-at-large, Paul Kelly.

The Kelly question

In July 2015, Paul Kelly wrote a thoughtful piece expressing his concerns that the advent of same-sex marriage would result in a loss of freedom for people of faith.

His argument was respectful, considered and free of judgment about gay and lesbian Australians. If there is an intellectual opposition to same-sex marriage, it has been articulated by Paul Kelly, and his arguments are worth reflecting on.

In his words:

> "The central issue in any Australian recognition of same-sex marriage remains almost invisible – whether the state's re-definition of civil marriage will authorise an assault on churches, institutions and individuals who retain their belief in the traditional view of marriage.
> "It seems to this point that none of the proposals for same-sex marriage or related policy prescriptions are satisfactory laws for passage by the Australian parliament. The real issue is conceptually simple – it is whether same-sex marriage will deny conscience rights to much of the population. The alternative is a new spirit of tolerance guaranteed by law where same-sex marriage sits in parallel with undiminished religious liberty.
> "The omens are not good. As the years advance there has been virtually no debate about the real issues surrounding same-sex marriage. The campaign for change is strong and tactically brilliant based on the ideological slogan "marriage equality", one of the most effective slogans in many decades."[69]

He went on:

> "If the Australian parliament intends to create a legal regime with this consequence then the law-makers must justify this to the people and explain how such calculated intolerance leads to a better society. The legalisation of same-sex marriage means the laws of the state and the laws of the church will be in conflict over the meaning of the most important institution in society. This conflict between the civil and religious meaning of marriage will probably be untenable and marked by litigation, attempts to use anti-discrimination law and entrenched bitterness. But an effort ought to be made to make it tenable on the basis of mutual tolerance."

Kelly expresses three key arguments. First, religious liberty and personal belief are equally important in our national life. Second, protections must exist for those individuals and institutions that, for conscience reasons, cannot endorse activities that support same-sex marriage. And third, no penalties must apply to those who act according to their conscience.

I agree with Paul Kelly that we have not considered how we can reconcile the right of one group to live out the tenets of their faith and the desire of an excluded group to receive equal treatment before the law.

We cannot replace one prejudice with another. As Northwestern University law professor Thomas Berg has said, "*When same-sex couples are told they will receive no more than toleration of their private behavior, they are asked to keep their identities significantly in the closet. But when traditionalist religious believers are told to keep their beliefs to themselves, or that it is not proper to follow them in the context of social services or the commercial marketplace, they too are told to keep their identities in the closet.*"[70]

When religious people are forced to vacate the public space we lose the virtues and the social capital they bring to it. Equally, when gay and lesbian couples are denied the full opportunities of citizenship, we also lose something of the joy and virtue they can bring to our community life.

The challenge is to navigate the conflicting views of marriage that are before our country.

Religious people see marriage as a religious institution ordained by God, and non-religious people see it as secular and, personal, and the right to marry as a derivative of citizenship. The historic truth is that under Australian law, the institution of marriage reflects both views.

Until recently, both the church and the state have benefited from this arrangement. In the words of Professor Perry Dane, "*The church has relied on the state to give juridical form to marriage, but the state has relied on the religious valence of marriage to give the institution meaning and depth.*"[71]

For religious people, marriage is considered a sacrament, or an act of consecration before God. It has not been argued that this act of consecration is annulled by others who choose not to be consecrated. This is because there is an implicit acceptance by religious people of the rights of people to choose civil marriage, and a belief that marriage is good for all. Yet opponents of same-sex marriage argue the exact opposite when it comes to same-sex couples.

According to this worldview, the atheist who might mock God is welcomed to the institution because the Christian understands that marriage is good, yet the gay or lesbian couple who seeks God's blessing and their country's support for their relationship finds the door shut.

How do we resolve the conflict between religious and non-religious people on this issue?

We can do so as adults, and with wisdom. It requires us all to walk a mile in another's shoes. It is only by doing so that we can appreciate that challenges of identity run deep within us all. Identity matters.

In the case of *Obergefell v Hodges*, a group of four legal scholars and a policy analyst presented an amici brief to the United States Supreme Court addressing the question of whether protection of religious liberty was a reason to prohibit same-sex marriage, or whether instead the Court could fully protect same-sex marriage and religious liberty:

> *"The proper response to the widely avoidable conflict between gay rights groups and religious liberty is to protect the liberty of both sides.*
> *"Both sexual minorities and religious minorities make essentially parallel clams on the larger society."*

It goes on to say that, *"Both sexual orientation and religious faith, and the conduct that follows from each, are fundamental to human identity. Both same-sex couples and religious organisations and believers committed to traditional understandings of marriage, face hostile regulation that condemns their most cherished commitments as evil."*

The question we must ask ourselves is how does this apply to Australia?

Does it mean that a Pentecostal taxi driver has the right to throw a gay couple out of his cab? Or does it give a restaurant owned by a Muslim the right to turn away a lesbian couple? The answer is clearly no. We operate our marketplace free of discrimination. All people, no matter their age, religion, sex, sexuality, or race have the same right to live their lives free of discrimination and condemnation. This is a settled question in our national life.

But should a Catholic school or church be compelled to hire out a hall or a chapel for a same-sex wedding? Will an Anglican teaching hospital be required to provide health information on gay sexual health? Will we require a Muslim relationship-counselling service to offer the service to same-sex couples? Will we require Catholic adoption agencies to offer adoption places to same-sex couples?

Naturally, the debate becomes more nuanced where public funds are involved. However, in Victoria we have seen what can happen. At the time of writing, the Andrews Government is requiring adoption agencies, including those operated by churches, to offer their services to same-sex couples. Consequently, the Catholic Church is considering withdrawing its adoption service from Victoria. The tragedy is, if the Church withdraws from this public space, the only losers will be children in orphanages in far-flung countries. Through the actions of the Andrews Government, we see a reflection of Paul Kelly's warning.

We see in the Andrews Government decision the ascendency of 'illiberal liberals' who are seeking to replace one community worldview with another. Of course gays and lesbians should have access to adoption services, as should Catholics and every other group in society. It is false to argue that we advance the cause of liberty by stripping liberty from one group in the name of freedom for another.

However, the response of conservatives should not be to engage in the same refusal to reflect on or debate these issues, or to pursue a retaliatory view of the world that sees us stuck in our ideological corners and refusing to engage in the substantive issues of the debate. If conservatives do that, how are we any different from the 'illiberal liberals'? We must stay engaged in the debates that shape our country and its freedoms.

The Andrews Government's action on adoption reflects my deepest lament about public discourse. In the age of social media, politics has become more polarised. We have lost the art of conversation and the willingness to negotiate with others. The most strident position is the one that is most rewarded. It is a time when we seek to prove our virtue by questioning that of another's. However, this is a false virtue. As Ernest Hemmingway once warned, *"There is nothing noble in being superior to your fellow man; true nobility is being superior to your former self"*.

By losing our discourse, we are losing our capacity to make nuanced decisions and deliver outcomes that preserve our national unity.

If we allow same-sex couples access to civil marriage, how do we ensure that this decision protects the freedom, liberty and identity of Australians who for religious reasons do not support same-sex marriage?

Some have argued that the way to protect religious liberty while allowing same-sex marriage is to relax the existing anti-discrimination laws that make it an offence to discriminate on the basis of sexuality.

Proponents of this view point to the United States and the case of Arlene's Flowers. In this case, a 71-year-old florist refused to provide flowers for a same-sex wedding, even though she had provided the couple with flowers for years. The florist argued before the Court that her objection was not towards the same-sex couple (who were long-term customers), but the marriage itself. The Court found that the florist had broken the local law and ordered her to pay the legal costs of the gay couple and a $1,001 fine. The florist said the ruling would send her broke.

Senator Penny Wong has made the observation that it would be madness to dragoon a hostile caterer or a disapproving photographer into a same-sex marriage for fear of getting overcooked main courses or blurry pictures. Her argument is that in Australia it is not a significant issue, and the market will sort this out.

I agree with Senator Wong that Australia is culturally different from the United States and that cases such as that involving Arlene's Florist will be few and far between. However, the market won't sort it out, because the law does not allow for informal arrangements whereby florists, cake-makers, chauffeurs and wedding planners can excuse themselves from a wedding on religious grounds.

We can see how this will play out. A Jewish cake-maker informally tries to excuse herself from making a wedding cake, citing her religious beliefs. The couple, in the midst of joyously preparing for their wedding, is deeply offended, and writes about it on social media. The post goes viral, the media pick it up, and the community debates the rights and wrongs of both parties. There are threats of boycotts and counter-boycotts, and somehow we are all left a little diminished by the squabble.

Tim Wilson, when he was Human Rights Commissioner, argued that the way to deal with matters such as this is to separate religious and civil marriage. A law could be drafted that protects religious freedom while avoiding unjust discrimination against same-sex couples. The law would simply require that any wedding service provider announces up-front the marriage tradition or traditions for which they provide services.

While I understand what Tim Wilson is trying to achieve, I struggle with his solution. It is too broad. On most wedding days there are two separate events – the wedding ceremony and the wedding reception.

Even if a couple is religious, a wedding reception is not a religious event. A wedding reception is a celebration of family and friends and it should be protected like any other celebration. A same-sex wedding reception is no different from any other wedding reception. There are speeches, laughter, a few tears, drinks and dancing. The fact that it is a lesbian or gay couple should not influence the decision of a caterer or reception centre on whether or not to accept the booking.

In the provision of services in the market place, people of faith are not the arbiters of other people's morals. At a typical wedding, the caterer does not ask if this is a second, third or fourth wedding for the bride or groom, nor does the florist ask if the groom has any AVOs out from an earlier relationship, or if the bride is marrying her fourth elderly husband in 10 years, or if the wedding enables either the bride or the groom to obtain Australian citizenship.

Our religious observance should regulate our own behaviour and outlook, rather than seeking to regulate those of other. There is no reason why gay and lesbian wedding celebrations should be subject to the moral scrutiny of another.

Where there is a case for a 'carve-out' from anti-discrimination laws is allowing people of faith to disqualify themselves from participating in or supporting a same-sex wedding ceremony. Religious people should be able to argue that a same-sex wedding is not in keeping with their religious tenets. They could argue that they believe that *'marriage is given by God'* and that to participate in such a ceremony cuts to the heart of their faith. In this case, we should allow people an exemption from providing services for a ceremony on the basis of their religion. This exemption should include civil celebrants, many of who are former priests, nuns and ministers.

There is a consistency in putting the case for same-sex marriage and for allowing people the right to exclude themselves from offering a service to a same-sex marriage ceremony, and it is my belief that there is a need for greater respect of our different identities. As the amici brief in the case of *Obergefell v Hodges* puts it, "*No one can have a right to deprive others of their important liberties as a prophylactic means of protecting their own.*"

We should be encouraging a culture of mutual respect. In this case, the person of faith and the same-sex couple are all trying to live a life worthy of their conscience. Through no fault of their own, their moral compasses are bringing them all into a difficult space.

We need to move this debate away from the 'click-baiters' who seek to enflame every dispute into an 'outrage'. Mostly, it's ordinary people trying to navigate their consciences in the best way they know how. While this answers the direct question about religious freedom and same-sex marriage, it does not answer the concern of Paul Kelly that some will use the change in the law as a lever to restrict religious freedom.

Increasingly, many are questioning the legitimacy of religious organisations in our national life. The essence of religion is that humanity does not have all the answers, and there is a purpose in our existence – and in understanding our limitations, a moral foundation was created for our world. As a conservative, I wonder what the world will be like without a sustaining faith. It is, as Paul Kelly writes, one of the serious questions of our age.

It can't be denied that religion is seen as increasingly suspect by a rational world. Along with that, the moral authority of the churches is no longer unquestioned, and given the revelations of recent times, that is not necessarily a bad thing. We must ask, what will this mean for people of faith? Will it result in increasing pressure to restrict their religious identity to the church pew?

These are the questions of our times. Continuing to argue the case against gays and lesbians accessing civil marriage is not answering them. If anything, it undercuts the message of the church, because it puts the church at odds with the values it articulates.

Part of the answer to the challenge of navigating these times lies in the philosophy of Menzies, who argued that our unique separate identities when brought together become a greater, stronger and more tolerant whole. It is our differences that prove we are free.

If *'tolerance'* demands that we become intolerant of difference then it results in a drab conformity of belief, opinion and outlook. As Tony Abbott often said about our country, *"We have found unity in our diversity and strength in our differences."* Our differences should not be a source of alienation, but a celebration of our God-given uniqueness. That is what we must strive for.

During a time when nations as great as the United States and the United Kingdom are fraying, Australia must rebuild its belief in a shared citizenship whereby all Australians have the same rights and privileges to live out their lives as they see fit.

For people of faith to argue convincingly for this shared vision of an equal citizenship, they must live this value. Living this value includes accepting the rights of gay and lesbian Australians to access civil marriage as a civil right. Allowing other citizens to freely live out their identities is not a threat to the church. Indeed, arguing for a citizenship in which people are free to make their own choices and live out their own values is the very way to protect people of faith as they navigate an age in which they do not hold the dominant worldview.

7

Render unto God

Throughout my childhood, I was educated at Catholic schools. The Good Samaritan nuns were my teachers in primary school and the Augustinian priests in high school.

One of the most influential teachers in high school was my English and Latin teacher, Fr Senan Ward.

Fr Senan originally hailed from Ireland. However, he was not an austere Irish priest, but one who had a compelling intellect and carried his faith with a gentle ease. In his class, I learned that language was a gateway to understanding the world and its sufferings and joys.

In Year 8, we spent a term studying great speeches, including John F. Kennedy's Inaugural Address. I learned about the great speechwriter Ted Sorensen, who I would meet 30 years later.

While Fr Senan was a great teacher, parish priest and school chaplain, his most remarkable work was when he headed up the Catholic Church's AIDS ministry in Melbourne in the mid to late 1980s and early 1990s.

It was during a time when the HIV virus was devastating the gay community and when the disease meant fear, rejection and almost always, death. Fr Senan lived out the charge of the prophet Isaiah to be *"a repairer of the breach"*. He reached out to men who felt rejected by their faith, devastated by life and stigmatised by the worst possible disease. He lived out his Christian faith in a way that reminds us of the real work of the church.

For six years, Fr Senan prayed at the bedsides of men about to depart this life, worked with support groups, quietly redirected the proceeds of church offering plates to help pay medical bills and helped reconcile men with their families. If they wanted, he'd also reconcile men with their God who had never left them or forsaken them.

In his words, Fr Senan became just a *"broker for God"*. But a broker for God in the tradition of St Mary MacKillop, Doctor Sister Mary Glowrey and Maximilian Kolbe who saw their God in the people around them.

Fr Senan is still a pastor to this day, in the family Parish Church at Manly Vale, and as I reflect on his work, I can hear the echo of St Francis:

> "Lord, make me an instrument of your peace
> Where there is hatred, let me sow love;
> Where there is injury, pardon;
> Where there is doubt, faith;
> Where there is despair, hope;
> Where there is darkness, light;
> Where there is sadness, joy."

Every day, churches and religious organisations across Australia undertake the good work of the gospel. The Catholic Church educates over 760,000 students in over 1,700 locations[72], tends to thousands of patients in dozens of hospitals, and operates welfare centres and charities for migrants, the homeless, the abused and those who are not enjoying life's blessings. In other denominations, we see the same ethos reflecting the words of St Paul: *"Always seek to do good to one another and to all"*.

The religious faiths of our country have added 'salt' and 'light' to our national life. Long before Ben Chifley spoke of *"the light on the hill"* and Ronald Reagan spoke of *"the shining city on a hill"*, Christ called his followers to be *"the light of the world"* and *"the city on a hill that could not be hidden."*

But the light flickers – and the debate over same-sex marriage reflects a deeper challenge for the Church. How does the Christian church live out its values, when the world and some in its congregation, believe that it is not?

Losing our children

One of the unexpected outcomes of being a speechwriter to a prime minister is that you find yourself falling in love with your country. Writing for a prime minister requires you to immerse yourself in our national story.

Michael Gerson is one of America's most respected evangelical thinkers. As Chief Speechwriter to President George W Bush, he was, like me, speechwriter to a deeply conservative national leader. He has seen the good and the bad of the culture wars from the frontline.

Since leaving Bush's side, Gerson has become a columnist and is now speaking in his own voice, not writing for the voice of another. In a 2015 speech to evangelicals, Gerson warned that the focus of the American church on *"reclaiming America"* and *"building a moral majority"* has come at a great cost to the church.[73]

He argues that evangelicals have become *"the antithesis of grace"*, and that in seeking to force an agenda on others, the church has become *"a marginal interest group among many others."* Evangelicals have pursued and are pursuing a strategy that has failed. As he says, *"we are no longer the home team, but the away team."* The church has become known for the pursuit of its interests and rights, and in so doing has become just another lobby group.

Worse than losing the culture wars, evangelicals are losing their own children.

Mostly, the children of evangelicals believe in the values and words of Christ — they believe in grace, mercy, forgiveness, understanding and compassion, but have walked away from the church because they do not believe the church's actions reflect those values.

While the Australian church has not sought to exercise its political clout to the extent that the American church does, Gerson's analysis also holds true for Australia.

For a quarter of a century, the National Church and Life Survey (NCLS) has been undertaking a longitudinal study of Australia's churches. The churches fund the study as a means of helping them to understand the motivations and attitudes of the various demographics within their denominations and congregations.

Some 260,000 churchgoers participated in the last survey in 2011. The survey reported that congregations were ageing at a faster rate than the general population, with 23 per cent of church members aged over 70 years. According to the survey, *"In many churches ageing attendees are not being replaced by younger people."*

At the same time, the number of people who identify as Christian in the Australian community is falling. In 1991, the Census reported that 74 per cent of Australians identified as Christian, but by the 2011 Census this had fallen to 61 per cent.

According to the 2011 NCLS, a solid majority of church attendees do not support same-sex marriage, with the most solid opposition coming from people over the age of 65. In church attendees below the age of 19, it is only a small majority.

Church teachers argue that fidelity to the teaching of Christ is more important than popularity. They believe that marriage is an institution created by God. In the words of the traditional wedding ceremony, marriage is *"given by God"* and even if they wanted to change it, they couldn't.

This is where the disruption of Pope Francis is so significant, because the Pope is shifting the focus from the systems and structures of the church to the people within and outside it. He is saying that the church should preoccupy itself not with public doctrines, but with private mercies. It should not look inward, but outward. The status and reputation of the church should not be as important as the care and protection of its people.

Francis has reminded us that the carpenter from Galilee was always the friend of prostitutes and sinners, and he better understood the complexities of humankind than the clerics who spoke in the name of God.

In Francis's words, *"The proclamation of the saving love of God comes before moral and religious imperatives. Today sometimes it seems that the opposite order is prevailing.*[74]*"*

Francis points to a faith where God's love for people triumphs over the systems, structures and church teachings that seem immovable. As he said about gay and lesbian people, *"Tell me, when God looks at a gay person does he endorse the existence of the person in love or reject and condemn this person? We must always consider the person."*

As Francis has identified, the challenge for the modern church is not to demand greater submission to ecclesiastical authority, but to more fully understand and embrace the human experience.

All too often, Christians have embraced a faith that embodies the virtues of grace, mercy, forgiveness, selflessness and community, but whose teachings about the lives of gays and lesbians seem to be glaringly at odds with these values. If sexual orientation is as natural as breathing, what does this say of God? If God is the creator, then surely he is the creator of all? He does not make mistakes.

These are questions that only the churches and their congregations can answer. If there is fidelity to the teachings of Christ – then these values must seep through every pore of the church.

My instinct is that the history of the church leans to grace. The church does not fail when it chooses the path of grace, nor does it fail when it makes decisions consistent with its values.

While marriage and love did not become the norm in society until about a century and a half ago, the church has argued throughout its history that life-long commitment and sex are inextricably linked. They go together. The counter-culture, and the prevailing societal norm, is that you can have sex, and you can have love, but they need not go together.

In the debate over same-sex marriage, those arguing for a change in the law believe in the unity of sex, love and life-long commitment. Yet, the church is arguing that for gays and lesbians, they can't go together – because it is not sex and it is not love.

We see in this that the core values that the church seeks for society are being negated by its own arguments when it comes to gay and lesbian people.

Humanity can see the symphony of creation. We see the optimism of a sunrise and the daily goodbye of a sunset. We see creation reminding us through its beauty of our mortality, reminding us that we will pass. Yet, in our theology, which is the very study of God, there is not that unity. Instead, we are seeing the same legalism and the same ecclesiastical judgment of people that Jesus despised.

Hair-splitting and ideals

In 2012, the Senate invited Australians to make submissions on laws to allow same-sex marriage. This was the opportunity for the churches to put the case for the status quo.

It was a tricky assignment for the churches, because in making a submission to a secular institution, they had to use secular arguments.

They could not say *"marriage is given by God"* and that they did not believe the government had the right to change it. To do so would have invited the response that under the Australian Constitution, the government cannot impose any religious test.

Instead, the churches sought to use logic and rationality but in doing so, they exposed the flaws in their arguments.

In answering the arguments they raised, I don't seek to ridicule the churches, because I admire the work they undertake in our communities. I merely seek to challenge an institution I so admire to think again.

I admire the Salvation Army, which does the work of angels every day. When I think of the Salvos, I think of my great uncle who spent much of the Second World War in a Japanese POW camp. As far as I know, he had no religious faith, but he always gave to the Salvos and bought a *War Cry* because he saw the unstinting devotion of the Salvos to the Australian Digger.

The Salvos' argument against same-sex marriage is straight-forward, but it is also deeply flawed. In the words of their submission, *"In spite of changing lifestyle and values, the family unit – father, mother and children – is still the ideal institution in contemporary Australian life."*[75]

When I look through the words of Jesus, I never see him pointing to *"the ideal"*. Most of us waste too much mental energy trying to work out whether we are normal, or match the ideal.

By the Salvos' own words, Christ himself does not measure up to their definition of ideal. After all, he was a single man who apparently supported his widowed mother.

I am part of a family that has a mother, father and two children, but our virtue is not determined by our structure or by our genders. Our virtue is determined by how we treat each other.

If we strive for an ideal, we will find that it never lasts. Families are dynamic institutions and how we function and relate to each other changes with time. Ten to fifteen years ago, my family changed. Our Christmas lunches were genial, relaxed affairs, then within a short period of time, Sarah and I had two children, and my sister and brother-in-law had three. Family events became loud, joyous and chaotic as five new family members asserted themselves within our ranks. Our family is changing again, as these young children become teenagers and my parents grow much older.

No family is ideal, but that's the beauty of families. We accept each other for who we are and we commit ourselves for the long haul. That is where we find family's strength.

In its submission to the Senate, the Australian Catholic Bishops Conference said, *"Families are small communities in themselves on which the wider community is built and they are the main place in which children are socialised to take their place in the wider community."*[86]

Most people, myself included, agree with this sentiment wholeheartedly. In fact, it is this sentiment that prompts me to ask, does it weaken a family when an adult daughter is asked by the man she has been dating for a long period of time to marry her? Assuming he is kind, caring and brings joy to her life, we would say no. He is a welcome addition to the family. What if it wasn't a 'he' she had been dating but a 'she'? Surely the same answer applies – as long as she is kind, caring and brings joy to the daughter's life, then the addition strengthens the family.

Families will still remain small communities, and same-sex parents, like heterosexual parents, will love, nurture and support their children as they take their place in the world. Just as importantly, parents with gay and lesbian children will be able to point those children towards loving, lifelong relationships that are affirmed and strengthened by the institution of marriage.

The most peculiar argument put by the churches against same-sex marriage came from the Anglican Synod of Sydney. The Synod argued that *"Presently a man, whatever his sexual orientation, has the legal capacity to marry a woman, and a woman, whatever her sexual orientation and gender identity, has the legal capability to marry a man. A person's sexual orientation and gender identity is irrelevant to their legal capacity to marry."*[77] As my children might say, "Huh?"

In other words, according to the Synod, it is perfectly fine for gays to marry lesbians, for bisexuals to marry someone of the opposite gender, for transgender men to marry women, or for transgender women to marry men, but it's not fine for a gay man to marry a gay man or a lesbian to marry a lesbian. In this argument, we see legalistic word games that *'do not consider the person'*.

More recently, the Moderator of the Presbyterian Church of Australia, the Right Reverend David Cook, put his concerns about same-sex marriage after a meeting with Malcolm Turnbull. The Moderator wrote, *"Changing that Act will change society; genderless marriage will lead to genderless families, no more mothers and fathers, just parents; genderless living will be used to encourage children to choose whichever gender they would like to be."*[78] No mums and dads! That's a new one.

Same-sex marriage has already occurred in many countries. There are still mums, there are still dads, and there are still children getting tucked in at night. For the 99 per cent of families with a mum and dad, or just a mum or a dad, nothing changes. For the small number of children who have same-sex parents, same-sex marriage just means that their parents can get married.

Secular and religious fundamentalism

If there is a group of people attracted like no other to the debate over same-sex marriage it is fundamentalists. Ironically, they don't seek debate, as they are the group least likely to engage in heartfelt reflection and in listening to an alternative point of view. I'm not just referring to religious fundamentalists, but to secular fundamentalists as well.

The secular fundamentalist and the religious fundamentalist are very similar, although they would both furiously deny it. They draw certainty from a fixed worldview, see non-conforming groups as a threat, and believe that the world needs to discard worldviews that are dissimilar to their own.

There is a strain of secular fundamentalism in modern life. Like the great 'isms' of the 20th century, they seek to destroy every error and remove from public life any who do not conform. These fundamentalists congregate on Twitter and the word 'Abbott' draws them out like BBQ meat can draw out a hungry pet. They are found on social media sharing Fairfax, BuzzFeed and Guardian stories as though they are sacred texts that the world needs to see. To them, no good can come from conservatives, from liberals or from people of faith.

When tragedies, atrocities and other dramatic events occur in the world, the religious and secular fundamentalist immediately uses it as proof of their own worldview. They will point to a natural disaster and quietly whisper the words 'climate change' or 'sin' because they are certain they know the true cause of this event.

Fundamentalists are unable to embrace mystery, because mystery makes the world less certain. However, fundamentalism offers unthinking reassurance. In the words of Andrew Sullivan, it *"frees the troubled mind from the burdens of existential fear and everyday trembling"* and provides *"meaning and direction to those lost in a disorientating world."*[79]

Secular and religious fundamentalists have more in common with those they mock than they realise. In their own ways, they are afraid of the complexities of life – of people with different worldviews, of events that cannot be explained, of the absurdities and sufferings and joys that come to the most unlikely people.

At times, religious fundamentalists have also been at the edges of their society and their loyalty has been questioned. Yale Law Professor William Eskridge observes the tendency to demonise or scapegoat religious people:

> *"Specific tropes include warnings that the polity faces irrevocable decline because of corrosive forces within the society; depiction of the despised religious group as dirty, immoral, lecherous, subversive, disloyal, and militant, based upon unrepresentative examples or simple fabrications; and fixation on the ways in which the despised group is bent on 'recruiting' normal citizens, particularly the young."*[80]

As Eskridge points out, these views are similar to those held by earlier generations about gays and lesbians.

The challenge in this debate is that fundamentalists sit on both sides of the fence – unable to hear or see the truths they share and unable to acknowledge the areas where there is neither certainty nor settled fact. So voices are raised, unity is lost and we are all the poorer, because we are too afraid to listen to each other.

In recent times, the world has seen the excesses of Islamic fundamentalism. After the Paris bombings Time magazine made this observation of the Islamic fundamentalists and those who defied them:

> *"The Parisian way of life – the cosmopolitan way of life – is under attack, and the young are responding with a sort of joyful protest clinking glasses of wine on terraces and congregating in crowded bars. They know that death makes sense only once we have experienced life, with its happinesses large and faint, its mournings, its comprehensions*

and its absurdities. They know fanatics who detonate themselves may not fear death but they will never know what life really is. They know it is life itself terrorism is afraid of.'[81]

How terrifying it must be to be afraid of life. The terror they project onto others is the terror they feel themselves.

It is differences that make the fundamentalist afraid. They have a 'stranger danger' view of the world that sees danger in everyone who views the world differently from them. The result is that they view others as stereotypes, rather than as people.

The religious fundamentalist sees gays and lesbians as immoral, self-centred, irresponsible people whose very presence mock's God's intrinsic order, and the secular fundamentalist sees the religious person as bigoted and homophobic, angry at the world and demanding conformity to the God they serve. All too often, the loudest voices have the greatest influence on our public debate.

If I have one observation to share from watching our national debate from the prime minister's office, it is that we are all losing the capacity to walk in the shoes of others and to treat others as we would like to be treated.

As I write about walking in someone else's shoes, I think of Tom Uren and the speech Tony Abbott gave in the Parliament following his death. Tom Uren was one of Labor's most honoured sons, having served in the Parliament for more than 30 years. In his day, he was a fierce 'lefty' and spent his life arguing passionately for his side of politics. However, I can't help but admire the man.

Tom Uren was a boxer, with a boxer's face, and at the age of 20 he enlisted in the Australian Army during the Second World War. He spent his 21st birthday and the three that followed as a prisoner-of-war. He served with 'Weary' Dunlop, and endured the worst of humanity on the Thai-Burma Railway. On one occasion, a Japanese soldier was poised to throw an Australian soldier off a bridge, and Uren stood between them, risking his own life. As the end of the war approached, he witnessed the dropping of the atomic bomb. The experience of war made him a life-long pacifist. He lived by the words of Martin Luther King, *"Hate distorts the personality and scars the soul. It is more injurious to the hater than the hated."*

Even if you did not agree with his politics, there was something deeply Australian about Uren's life. It was a rugged life, that believed in something bigger than himself, and he was willing to fight for it, first in the Army, and then in the Parliament. He didn't pursue wealth, because it just didn't seem important. As Tony Abbott said in his parliamentary tribute, *"Tom Uren will always be remembered as more than simply a son of his party. He will be remembered as a great son of Australia."*[82]

Our shared challenge in the debate over same-sex marriage is to see the good in each other and to treat others with respect and decency. Seeking to walk a mile in another person's shoes does not make us weak, it makes us strong. It is not just hate that "scars the soul"; it is fear as well.

The fundamentalist is certain about their views, be they religious or political. However, faith is not about certainty. Faith is the absence of certainty, and it rests on the foundation of doubt.

Faith does not require us to banish difference, nor to stigmatise those we do not understand or dismiss and mock those who have a different worldview. Instead, it calls us to embrace life, to ask questions, to accept that we do not have all the answers and to see the good in others.

8

ANSWERING THE ARGUMENTS AGAINST SAME-SEX MARRIAGE

It was the philosopher Sidney Hook who said *"Before impugning an opponent's motives, even when they may rightly be impugned, answer his arguments."*

To answer someone's arguments is to show them respect. Answering an argument first requires that you listen to someone. It means putting yourself in another's shoes and trying to feel what they are saying.

I repeat – trying to *feel* what someone is saying.

Those who oppose same-sex marriage fear it. It's a feeling. For some, it's visceral. They fear that the foundations that they have long accepted as truths, even eternal truths, are being torn down. For them, same-sex marriage is another change in a society that no longer seems moored in the truths of faith. It is another sign that the teachings and foundations they were given as children no longer seem to matter.

Mostly, these fears aren't answered by rational arguments (although I will continue to put them) but by the good and quiet lives lived by gay and lesbian Australians.

They are answered by the lesbian neighbour who asks if you need something at the shops because she knows you are ill.

They are answered by the gay emergency services volunteer who helps you repair your house after a storm has struck.

They are answered by the transgender nurse who cares for your father as he succumbs to the ravages of cancer.

Our real-life experiences with gay, lesbian, bisexual, transgender and intersex Australians have revealed a truth that is also a paradox: we are all different, but we are all the same. We are all people who were once dust, are now flesh, and will become dust again.

As a conservative and as a Christian, I feel the pathos of the human condition. It is in my bones. Our time is fleeting, our capacities are incomplete and we all fall short of who we can be. If this is our condition, then the answer is grace towards each other because our journeys are harder than others imagine.

It is because of our daily interactions with people from all walks of life that the fears of the past are washing away. We are living out the summation of the law and the prophets to do unto others as you would have them do unto you.

The change in attitudes towards gay and lesbian Australians is one of the most remarkable changes that has occurred over the past 25 years. It has not occurred because of political movements, although as in every part of life, it has its activists, nor has it occurred as the result of denunciations or demonstrations. Rather, it is the result of the countless interactions Australians have with gay and lesbian people every day.

The old prejudices are confronted by a radical thought. It is a whimsical whisper at first, and then it slowly takes hold, until almost unbelievably we come to see our similarities through our differences. We see others not through the lens of a label or a brand of sexuality; rather, we see them as fully human.

We realise that the lives of others are as little, as mundane, as joyous and, at times, as sad as our own. We come to understand that we all yearn to love, to be loved and to be accepted for who we are.

Life teaches us that there comes an open-hearted grace from

truly knowing another person. When we see and hear the honest struggles of another, when we see their limitations and the resulting determination to stretch them, and when we see them doggedly face the undeserved knocks and circumstances of life, we see a reflection of our own humanity.

In putting forward the answers to the arguments against same-sex marriage, I am not putting forward political talking points to be hammered away at relentlessly, day after day. I am putting forward the arguments with which to respectfully answer your neighbour.

The words and arguments are only as powerful as the tone behind them.

This debate is different from most political debates that occur in our country. All too often, political parties develop talking points that are principally about putting your own case rather than engaging with the arguments of your opponents. They are about ignoring your opponents' arguments rather than answering them. There are reasons for this. Studies have shown that political headway is made when a candidate is arguing their own issues and not those of their opponents. In other words, you pick the terrain you fight on.

But that approach doesn't work on same-sex marriage, because there is only one question and one issue: do you support changing the law to allow same-sex marriage?

Thus the rules are different. In putting the case for change, the arguments against change need to be answered one by one.

We must show respect for those who disagree by answering their arguments, rather than ignoring them.

Hectoring, questioning their motives or mocking their faith won't work. After all, do these tactics ever convince people to change their minds? And frankly, what does it say of us if that is the extent of our ability to argue for change?

If there is a plebiscite, it will be won house by house, street by street, and suburb by suburb. It will be won by respectfully answering the questions and arguments of others.

The arguments against same-sex marriage

There are ten arguments used by those who do not support same-sex marriage. Some of them are not even about same-sex marriage, but as I have said to some of the politicians I have worked for, 'we don't get to choose what the voters are interested in'.

These are the arguments put forward by opponents of same-sex marriage:

1. Same-sex marriage is a third-order issue.

2. Marriage is an unchanging institution that should not be tampered with.

3. Changing the definition of marriage will undermine heterosexual marriage.

4. Same-sex marriage is unnatural (the anatomy argument).

5. You can't trust men to be faithful.

6. Children need a mum and a dad.

7. Churches will be forced to perform same-sex marriages and violate their religious traditions.

8. This is part of the 'slippery slope' and there will be unintended consequences of this change.

9. Same-sex unions can't be a marriage so let's support civil unions.

10. Australia is not ready for same-sex marriage – we should wait.

Let's answer these arguments one by one.

1. ARGUMENT: Same-sex marriage is a third-order issue

Saying '*It's just not important*' – is the simplest way to oppose same-sex marriage without explaining why.

To dismiss an issue because it doesn't affect you doesn't quite cut it in a democracy.

The ABS does not survey people on their sexuality (nor would we want them to), but most estimates put the number of gay and lesbian people at somewhere between 3 and 4 per cent of the population.

Australia has a population of 24 million,[83] which means there are likely to be something in the order of 720,000 to 960,000 Australians who are (or are likely to be) gay, lesbian, bisexual, transgender, or intersex. For simplicity's sake, let's say the number is at the halfway point of these two figures – 840,000 Australians.

These 840,000 Australians all have families. They have mums and dads, grandmothers and grandfathers, sisters and brothers, and many have sons and daughters. As marriage is the legal way by which partners become kin, all of these families will benefit from the right to admit new members to their families.

So how does the 'third-order issue' that directly affects 840,000 Australians directly and millions of others indirectly compare with the size of other communities and issues in our country?

The number of Australians attending university is 823,000.[84]

The number of Australians receiving a veterans service pensions is 64,800.[85]

The number of Australian children in child care is 662,000.[86]

The number of Australians serving in the Australian Defence Force is 78,100.[87]

The number of Indigenous Australians is 669,900.[88]

The number of nurses and doctors in Australia is 327,400.[89]

The number of older Australians who are living in aged care is 180,300.[90]

No one ever argues that we shouldn't help veterans, or age pensioners, or children in child care, or Aboriginal and Torres Strait Islanders. No one ever says that helping them is a 'third order issue'. In terms of the number of people it potentially affects, same-sex marriage is a first order issue.

Countries can 'walk and chew gum' at the same time. We have the capacity to help all our people, and at times we also have the capacity to pay additional attention to an issue.

In 2015, the House of Representatives passed 180 bills. Governments and parliaments can do more than one thing at once. Both sides of the debate agree that Australia has been discussing this issue for 15 years now and the time for a definitive vote has come.

The 'third-order issue' argument does not stack up.

2. ARGUMENT: Marriage is an unchanging institution that should not be tampered with

As detailed in Chapter 4, marriage has changed over time.

Marriage is about love, not finances; people make their own choices to marry rather than relying on the decision of their parents; different races can intermarry; Indigenous people can marry without asking for permission; women are considered the equals of men; family law considers the rights of women and children; Australian children as young as 12 years of age can no longer marry; almost three-quarters of all marriages are the result of civil ceremonies and divorce does not need a guilty party. These are just some of the changes that have occurred over time, and they are all changes that we now take for granted.

The Commonwealth Marriage Act has changed 20 times since it was first introduced, and it can change again.

Marriage changes as society changes. This is what ensures that marriage stays relevant and that it remains strong.

3. ARGUMENT: Changing the definition of marriage will undermine heterosexual marriage

It is argued that somehow, heterosexual self-esteem and self-understanding will be devastated if gays and lesbians are considered their equals before the law.

The Conservative Prime Minister of New Zealand, John Key, answered this argument best when his government was legislating for same-sex marriage. He said, *"If two gay people want to get married, then I can't see why it would undermine my marriage to Bronagh."*[91]

One has to ask where the threat is, for those who support same-sex marriage don't seek to overthrow marriage, but seek to join it, to honour it and to strengthen it. They believe in the values and benefits of marriage that they have seen through the lives of their parents, their siblings and their friends.

The gentle evolution of marriage over the past 200 years has strengthened the institution.

Rather than threaten heterosexual marriages, same-sex marriage seeks to include gays and lesbians in a conservative view of relationships. Conservatives believe that stable relationships lead to stable societies.

The strangest part of the argument that same-sex marriage will hurt heterosexual relationships is that it mirrors the 'culture of offence' that conservatives rightly condemn.

The 'culture of offence' wants to stop carols at Christmas because it will somehow offend others, and it is the 'culture of offence' that thinks it is acceptable for students of other religions or nationalities to sit down or walk out of a school assembly during the playing of the National Anthem. We are highly bewildered by the concept that freely living our lives and expressing our beliefs should be deemed to offend or diminish others.

If we believe in the orthodoxy of people living free lives and not having to apologise for who they are or what they believe in, why should heterosexuals take offence at homosexual relationships? There is no offence.

Same-sex marriage doesn't undermine heterosexual relationships any more than Christmas carols undermine Jewish holidays, or the National Anthem of Australia undermines Muslim identity.

4. ARGUMENT: Same-sex marriage is unnatural (The anatomy argument)

The media commentator, Piers Akerman describes the anatomy argument this way: *"Among humans, marriage is the joining of a man and a woman, different sexes, one hole… At the simplest, a marriage is reflected by the relationship between a nut and a bolt. A single nut is not much use. Neither is a bolt, but the two in tandem as they are designed to be used, form an effective fastener. Two nuts do not make it, nor two bolts. Try to put them together and they don't marry."*[92]

It's a similar argument to that used by Nationals MP, Andrew Broad, who says, *"I think a bicycle is not a tricycle, and relationships can have different names. I can put the rams in a paddock and they might mount one another, but no lambs will come out."*[93]

Some have rushed to condemn both men. Nuts and bolts; sheep and rams; bicycles and tricycles; where will it end?

I have to confess, I'm not offended by the arguments because they represent an honest view – even if it is an incomplete one. They have expressed in simple, straight-forward words what others have hidden behind more obtuse language. Often, I see more honesty in arguments made with candour than in those cloaked in language deemed to be socially acceptable.

Both men put forward the same argument, even if their analogies are totally different. The essence of this argument is that we have either a penis or a vagina – and that is all that matters when you are producing children. In other words, it is our capacity to produce children that makes marriage special.

According to this worldview, the special status of marriage is derived from children. Yet this does not reflect our lived experience. Children are a blessing, there is no question about that, but love, joy, humour, support, compassion and mercy can also be found in homes without children.

One day my children will leave home. Will that mean that my marriage has no purpose, simply because our children are adults? Or is the relationship I have with Sarah something more? Does its meaning and value come from a shared life, with its highs and lows, its struggles and triumphs?

I love my children, but I have seen relationships as meaningful as ours in couples without children.

In its ground-breaking judgment on same-sex marriage, the Supreme Court of Massachusetts made this observation:

> "*It is the exclusive and permanent commitment of the marriage partners to one another, not the begetting of children, that is the sine qua non of civil marriage.*"[94] (*Sine qua non* is the indispensable and essential action or ingredient.)

We have all known and seen marriages that prove that truth. In my own family, I think of an aunty and uncle. Forty years ago, in the first years of their marriage, my aunty was struck down with Hodgkin's lymphoma. In those days, the treatments were brutal. But, as she reminds me, she lived, and others she met didn't, and she will always be grateful for her treatment. However, the result of the treatment was that she could not have children.

My aunty would have been the most wonderful mother. Over the years she showered her nephews and nieces with kindness and support. Each of us feels that we are her favourite. She is also our favourite aunty, and is now joyfully demonstrating the same generosity and affection towards her dozens of great-nieces and great-nephews.

Can we truly accept the argument that her marriage to my uncle lost its meaning when the possibility of having children was gone? Or do we see the meaning of the marriage through a husband and wife supporting each other through one of life's most terrible trials?

Of course, the support and care of children is a reason for marriage, but it is not the sole reason. The foundation of marriage is not the children who may spring from it; it is the love and commitment that inspires the creation of those children.

Love and commitment can be found in people who are of childbearing age and in those who aren't. It is not our fertility that makes us suitable for marriage, it's our humanity.

Loving relationships are not about 'nuts and bolts'; they are about heart and soul. These attributes stand above gender; they are the essence of our humanity. Thus, gays and lesbians can have relationships as meaningful as heterosexuals. There is no reason to deny gay, lesbian, transgender and intersex Australians the opportunity and responsibility of marriage.

5. ARGUMENT: You can't trust men to be faithful

There is already a man in every heterosexual marriage. While some women might declare in frustration that *'all men are bastards'*, no one has argued that we should ban marriage because of men.

If you follow the 'you can't trust men' argument through to its logical conclusion, you discover that it's only an argument for lesbian marriage.

However, this argument reflects an unspoken code. It's a form of 'dog whistle' that draws out prejudice without saying anything prejudicial.

The argument is code for saying that you can't trust gay men because they are promiscuous, selfish and behave like out of control teenagers. In this argument, an old stereotype about gays is dusted off and hidden in an argument about all men.

It is a case of looking at the speck in your brother's eye rather than the log in your own. The argument about some men can easily be the argument about most men.

Some argue that many single men (both heterosexual and gay) are promiscuous and what changes them, partly or wholly, is marriage, or the promise of marriage. The yearning for intimacy finally triumphs over the yearning for immediacy.

Many men 'sow wild oats' but men can change, and mostly they change because of marriage.

The promise and hope of marriage offers men the pathway to settling down, to becoming responsible for others and to finding joy in their spouse and family. It is another reason why marriage should be available to all.

6. ARGUMENT: Children need a mum and a dad

Marriage is no longer the means by which couples are sanctioned to have children. People can have children whether they are married or not. In a theoretical sense, this is not a debate about children; it's a debate about the legal rights of adults. However, at a practical level, we know that marriage and children are tied together in our thinking on this issue.

Some who oppose same-sex marriage do so because they believe it will encourage gays and lesbians to have children. On this assumption, the boat has already sailed. Gays and lesbians have been raising children for a while now, and this will continue to occur whether same-sex marriage is legislated or not.

However, we should still answer the underlying question – is this a good thing?

Concerns about the welfare of children are underpinned by two assumptions. First, that marriage is a licence, or the approval of the state, to have children. Second, children need gender role models provided by a mother and a father. Answering these two assumptions is critical if we are to demonstrate that the welfare of children is not being compromised by allowing same-sex marriage.

Marriage is a licence for children

For centuries, marriage was a licence to have children, and in some places in the world, it still is.

When society considered marriage as a licence to have children, it stigmatised those without such a licence. We witnessed shotgun weddings, forced adoptions, the separation of mothers and their children, and a shaming of people that still washes through our land to this day.

Marriage is no longer a licence to have children. That is not to say that children do not benefit from the emotional, social and economic supports provided by marriage; they do.

Children are the beneficiaries of marriage. A stable, loving and supportive home provides an emotional foundation for life. However, we have learned that when governments, or charities, or churches, or families prescribe who can or cannot have children, upheaval and trauma inevitably follow.

In the history of our nation, we have made three National Apologies: to the Stolen Generations, for Forced Adoptions and to Child Migrants. All three apologies had a common theme; they spoke of the heartache of children separated from their birth parents.

As then Opposition Leader Tony Abbott said at the National Apology for Forced Adoptions, "*We turned what should been the wonderful experience of new life into something filled with shame. Instead of love, there was reproach; instead of support, rejection; instead of celebration, silence; and instead of justice, there was wrongdoing.*"[95]

We have learned from our mistakes, and marriage is no longer a licence to have children. We understand that the licence to have children is found in the love of their parents.

Today men and women are making their own choices about how to raise their children – in marriage, in de facto relationships, with same-sex partners and sometimes alone. According to the ABS, 34 per cent of Australian children are now born outside of wedlock.[96] Twenty years ago, it was 22 per cent.

Gays and lesbians are already having children. Some are adopting, while others are using surrogates or sperm donors. The advent of same-sex marriage will not change this, nor will its delay, stop it.

At the time of the 2011 Census, there were 6,300 children living in same-sex couple households. While this might represent a transformation in attitudes it does not, nor will it, represent a significant change in the demographic makeup of parenting across Australia.

As the ABS noted:

> "*Children in same-sex couple families make up only one in a thousand of all children in couple families (0.1%). The vast majority of these children (89%) were in female same-sex couple families. Children in same-sex couples may have been born into a previous opposite-sex relationship of one of the partners, or conceived with the help of reproductive technology, adopted, or fostered in a same-sex relationship.*"[97]

It is unlikely that same-sex marriage will change the make-up of Australian families. It is a matter of statistics. Gay and lesbian people make up about 3.5 per cent of the population. Surveys of gays and lesbians in committed relationships have found that about 15 per cent of them want to have children, but not all of those who want to have children will take the necessary steps to do so. When you multiply these fractions and probabilities, the number of children in Australia with same-sex parents still ends up in the vicinity of somewhere between one in every 400 and one in every 800. In other words, just one or two children in every primary school.

Those who oppose same-sex marriage have expressed concern for these children. We know that children thrive in loving and stable families. So my question for those who oppose same-sex marriage is, why prevent the parents of these children from getting married?

One of my responsibilities in Tony Abbott's office was the correspondence system. Each year, anywhere from 150,000 to 200,000 letters and emails are sent to the Prime Minister (whoever he or she may be), and we had a highly developed triage system that allowed us to identify letters that were out of the ordinary or needed personal attention.

Most weeks, the Prime Minister would receive letters from children with same-sex parents asking if their parents could marry. What struck me from reading about 100 of these letters is that the children felt they were missing out on something that other families had.

I understand politics well enough to know that some of those letters were organised by parents – when eight-year-olds start quoting international comparisons or the letter is leaked to *Fairfax* or *The Guardian,* you know it was Mum or Dad who was the instigator. But mostly, they were handwritten letters, with plenty of spelling mistakes, gaps in logic and a belief that prime ministers were all powerful. For these children, marriage meant affirming their family and giving it a standing amongst their schoolmates and community that it does not currently have. These kids were right; marriage is good for families, and it would be good for their families.

Marriage is no longer a licence to have children, but it is a foundation for families. It provides children with confidence that their parents are committed to each other and to them. The children of same-sex parents know this, their parents know this, and strengthening these families is in all our interests.

Children and parents

In any debate, we should always start at a point where both sides agree. In this debate, both sides agree that parenting is a two-person job.

I admire the women, and the men as well, who through circumstances beyond their control find themselves raising a child or children by themselves. As Tony Abbott once reminded us, *"The harder something is, and few things are harder than raising a child alone, the more people should have had our support, not our judgment."*[98]

Emotionally, nothing tests a person more than parenting. Barack Obama once described the joy and anxiety of parenthood as *"the equivalent of having your heart outside of your body all the time, walking around."*[99]

Even when everything is going well, parenting is unrelenting. It demands and tests you, but equally, there is nothing that compares to the joy that it can bring.

Beyond the mechanics of getting children to school, being there when they come home and helping them to get organised for activities, parenting is also the work of forging a child's character. Parents know that the job of producing well-adjusted young adults can at times involve a clash of wills. Children do not naturally think of others. Teaching children to look out for others, to be responsible and to make the right decisions is a long process. Parents are tested to their limits as the child they created looks them in the eye and yells "NO!"

Parenting is more than conception, but all too often this debate gets stuck on conception. First and foremost, parenting is about the lifelong relationship between parents and their children, and the ability of parents to bring up happy and healthy children.

The welfare of children is always a legitimate discussion to have in any society.

Penny Wong has put the case that the argument about children is hurtful to families with same-sex parents because it pre-supposes that gays and lesbians are bad parents. I understand that argument. Just about every parent I know (no matter their sexual orientation) has a story about a 'bad parent' insinuation thrown their way. It might have been been a comment or just a look in the supermarket. It sends parents bonkers.

Same-sex parents are right to want to protect their family from unfounded insinuations, but there is also a responsibility to actively participate in the debate and to reassure people.

We should be able to discuss what gender means in families without having to make insinuations about the motives and character of lesbian and gay parents.

Like most other parents, gay and lesbian parents are their own harshest critics. They want what is best for their child, but they also know their own limitations and imperfections.

As children and teenagers, we are critical of our parents and the choices they make, but when we become parents, we realise that parents are trying to do their best given the circumstances and limitations they face.

Just like other parents, some lesbians and gays won't manage parenthood particularly well. Some will also bring their children into family settings that are already unstable. However, there is one legitimate question that many people have about same-sex parents that deserves an answer: can two parents of the same gender parent children as effectively as two parents of different genders?

The question of gender differences is best answered by the research of Dr Michael Lamb, who is a world-recognised authority on the role of fathers in the development of children. Dr Lamb has spent decades researching fatherhood, and has found that *"Fathers and mothers seem to influence their children in similar rather than dissimilar ways. Contrary to the expectations of many psychologists, including myself...the differences between mothers and fathers appear much less important than the similarities."*[100]

The research demonstrates that what mums and dads do is not that dissimilar:

> *"Not only does the description of mothering largely resemble fathering, but the mechanisms and means by which fathers influence their children also appear very similar to those that mediate maternal influences on children."*

He argues that what truly matters to children is having parents who are warm, nurturing and close to them. In every circumstance, a close, engaged and reliable parent is better than a distant, unpredictable or abusive one – and that holds, no matter what your gender.

Implicit in questions about same-sex parents is the fear that somehow homosexuals will reproduce homosexuals (even though one might joke and say that heterosexuals have been doing that for years) and that somehow the balance of sexualities might change.

If this were true, it would be worthy of reflection. We could then ask, does the balance of sexualities change? If so, does it matter? However, Lamb's evidence suggests that this debate won't be happening any time soon, if at all, with the research indicating that *"the sexual orientation of homosexual fathers does not influence the likelihood that their children will be homosexual, effeminate or maladjusted."*[101]

A study comparing the children of lesbians with those of heterosexuals also found *"no difference..with respect to favourite television programs, favourite television characters, or favourite games or toys. The research suggests the children of lesbian mothers develop patterns of gender-role behaviour that are much like that of other children."*[102]

In other words, gays and lesbians who parent children will produce children as energetic, joyous, naughty, loud and disobedient as any other couple.

Gender does not matter as much as we think it does. In the words of the research, *"very little about the gender of a parent seems to be distinctly important"*.

It's worth remembering that half a century ago people questioned the result of mixed marriages and what it would do to 'the stock of the races'. At the time, one southern judge in the United States argued that *"the offspring of these unnatural connections are generally sickly, effeminate, and they are inferior to the full blooded of either race in physical development and strength"*.[103]

The fears about parents from different races were wrong, and the fears about same-sex parents as just as wrong.

However, this is not to say that children don't need role models from their own gender. Of course they do. For generations, uncles and aunties, grandparents and extended families have stepped up to the plate when there has been no gender role model in the family home.

My wife's mother died when she was a young girl. Forty years on, there's not a day when Sarah does not think of her mum. She holds on to her limited memories of her mother like precious treasures.

As Sarah grew up, her two grandmothers and her aunties helped her to navigate her way through many of the issues that are unique to girls. They took her out to buy dresses and chat over milkshakes, they let her explore creativity in making clothes, and they helped her through the teenage years.

As well, Sarah spent more time with her father. Her dad is a practical man (unlike her husband), and she learned how to fix cars, repair roofs, and to be an all-round 'handy-woman'. She gravitated towards the adults who gave her love and attention. That is what counts, no matter who is parenting a child.

Gay and lesbian parents involve their extended families in the lives of their children, just like any other parents. Their children play with cousins and have sleepovers with aunties and uncles, and the extended family is involved in helping the children to understand what it means to be a good person and what it means to be a happy and well adjusted male or female. No matter what their sexuality, parents want what's best for their children. That is a universal truth.

What matters for children is that they have committed parents and a loving family. Marriage strengthens families, and the children of gay and lesbian parents will benefit from the protections that come from marriage.

7. ARGUMENT: Churches will be forced to perform same-sex marriages and violate their religious traditions.

This is an argument that is comprehensively answered in Chapter 6. To recap:

> Section 47 of the Marriage Act already allows a minister of religion who is a marriage celebrant to refuse to marry anyone on any grounds they see fit. No one is proposing any change to that provision.

Section 116 of the Constitution provides strong protection for religious freedom. The Constitution is unambiguous:

> **"Commonwealth not to legislate in respect of religion**
> *The Commonwealth shall not make any law for establishing any religion, or for imposing any religious observance, or for prohibiting the free exercise of any religion, and no religious test shall be required as a qualification for any office or public trust under the Commonwealth."*[104]

In almost all religions, marriage is a religious ceremony. If governments sought to overturn religious freedom in marriage, two things would happen. First, it would represent a giant intervention in the activities of Australia's religions that would play itself out at the ballot box.

Second, any law that sought to compel religious organisations to change their religious practices would be challenged and defeated in the High Court.

Even if a government wanted to compel religions to marry same-sex couples, they would have no legal power to do so. The power to bless a couple is within the gift of religious organisations, and no one is arguing for that to change.

8. ARGUMENT: This is part of the 'slippery slope' and there will be unintended consequences of this change

The slippery slope is not an argument, but a reflection of a deeper fear. In some ways the slippery slope is a harder argument to answer. It is the assertion that unforeseen consequences will be the result of changes to marriage without having to state explicitly what they are.

This is an old argument. It was put forward when married women were given property rights and when people of different races were allowed to marry. It is not a rational argument but an emotional one. It is a fear that the world will change into something unimaginable and the truths we hold dear will be discarded along the way.

Stability, certainty and tradition bring their comforts. They anchor us, but they were never meant to enslave us. Traditions are renewed and reinterpreted in accordance with the times we live in. If we believe, as conservatives do, that tradition, custom and institutions are the embodiment of centuries of wisdom, then we can see that 'the embodiment of wisdom' is a work in progress. That is why the 15 year debate on same-sex marriage has been a good thing. There has been no rush. The arguments have been tested. Other countries have made changes. Some like the United Kingdom made initial tentative moves with civil unions and then more confidently moved to marriage itself. The essence of the institution did not change. In our aspirations, it still represents our highest hopes, and in practice, it still strengthens the mortal frames of individuals through their journey in life.

Often, our fears blind us to our hopes and to the possibilities before us. During the first half of the 20th century there was a view that strong families needed to be homogenous. Many countries banned inter-racial marriages and marriages between different religions, even between different churches, were frowned upon. In addition, making women equal partners in marriage by giving them equal rights before the law, meant that marriage was no longer economic, social and emotional imprisonment for the woman who married the wrong man. Today, we wonder how people held such antiquated views of marriage and we understand that these changes have not made our families weaker; they have made them stronger.

Every change to marriage has been resisted. In every generation, there are people predicting that change will mean the end of marriage and the end of the family. Instead, the gentle incremental changes that occur in every generation have made marriage more resilient, more responsive to the changes that are occurring within society and more able to help us to navigate our shared lives.

Marriage is not on a slippery slope. Instead, it has gently changed with every new generation. These changes have not weakened marriage; they have made it as strong and as enduring as ever.

The slippery slope to polygamy

Sometimes, the slippery slope argument extends to the surreal.

The polygamy argument is one such example. Historically, polygamy has always been an institution that is male centred. It is also an institution based on male dominance, because it is about the husband taking multiple wives. I am yet to see an example of a wife taking multiple husbands.

It is an anachronism. Polygamy is a complexity that might have worked in an isolated, ancient community where a man provided protection for more than one woman. But it is not a model that works in the modern world where men and women are equals.

I can honestly say I am yet to meet a polygamous person. As we know from the same-sex marriage debate, changes to marriage require broad and deep support.

Andrew Sullivan argues that the changes that have occurred in Western countries regarding same-sex marriage are the direct result of Americans getting to know their gay and lesbian compatriots. US polls indicate that 78 per cent of Americans say they know a gay or lesbian person, which is triple the figure just a generation ago.[105] There is no evidence of a large, hidden polygamous population in our country. On the contrary, the evidence is that it is a historical anachronism.

On this issue, Australians with different sexualities might make a similar observation – I can only just manage one lifelong relationship; is anyone really suggesting two, three or four? No thanks.

There has been no movement towards marriage between three, four or five people overseas and there is no such movement here.

Marriage is between two people. Full stop. End of story.

This argument is a red herring. It does not stack up.

The slippery slope to bestiality

It was in 2012 that Coalition frontbencher Senator Cory Bernardi argued that same-sex marriage would eventually result in moves towards "consensual sexual relations between humans and animals" and human-animal marriages.

At the time, Senator Bernardi was a junior member of Tony Abbott's frontbench. Abbott repudiated Bernardi's comments and Bernardi subsequently resigned from the Coalition frontbench. He has been on the backbench ever since.

At a personal level, Bernardi is a likeable person, and it is difficult to reconcile the warm individual with such an offensive argument.

However, let's answer the argument, because someone, somewhere will run it again.

I have met thousands of people in life, but I am yet to meet a person who wants to marry their cat, their goldfish, the kangaroo in the back paddock, or their neighbour's sheep? It isn't happening. It won't happen.

Marriage is a contract, and animals don't sign contracts. Animals don't apply for jobs, they don't drive cars, they don't go to school and they don't read and write.

This is another argument that reflects fear rather than logic, and is based on an imaginary world rather than on reality.

None of the slippery slope arguments holds water.

No one wants to return to Biblical times when Jacob married Rachel and Leah, who were sisters, or when Lot's daughters got him drunk so that he could father their children, or when the patriarch Abraham married his half-sister Sarah.

It is unfair of me to draw that analogy, but I do so to make a point. In the same way in which it is unfair to argue that the followers of age-old religions want a return to incest, it is as unfair to equate Australians in healthy and loving same-sex relationships with wanting to marry an animal, a family member or multiple partners.

The slippery slope arguments should be left alone, because they are merely a means of casting dark insinuations about the character of other people.

The slippery slope to unintended consequences.

Conservatives believe in slow and evolutionary change rather than radical, revolutionary change. We do so because change always has unintended consequences.

Sometimes the consequences of a proposed change can be guessed, but mostly they catch us by surprise. That's not to say that unintended consequences can't be positive; many times they are.

However, Australia is not conducting a social experiment by considering same-sex marriage. Twenty-three countries have already welcomed same-sex marriage. Some, like the United Kingdom, moved in two steps, civil unions and then marriages, but increasingly it is one step.

There have been no negative unintended consequences. In these countries, the debate has ended. The circus tent has moved on. The culture wars on marriage are over, and everyone is quietly getting on with their lives.

The positive second-order consequences are washing through countries, communities and families. Teenagers who might be questioning their sexuality, are attending the weddings of a gay uncle or a lesbian cousin and are finding that their fears aren't as great as they imagined. Sons and daughters are hearing speeches of devotion at their weddings from their mums and dads as they welcome their child's spouse into their families. As well, children of gay parents are watching their parents marry and realising that their family is just as good as any other.

All weddings, religious or civil, remind us of an eternal truth:

> *"There is a time for everything, and a season for every activity under the heavens: a time to be born and a time to die, a time to plant and a time to uproot, a time to weep and a time to laugh, a time to mourn and a time to dance."*[106]

The lived experience is that allowing gay and lesbian people to marry strengthens their relationships and draws them closer to their families and loved ones.

This is a reflection of the best in the conservative ethos, and it is change that should be welcomed.

9. ARGUMENT: Same-sex unions can't be a marriage so let's support civil unions

I like this argument. I like it because it goes to the heart of why many people oppose same-sex marriage – and I like it because it is so easy to answer.

It's an argument best answered by a submission from the Australian Christian Lobby (ACL) on same-sex marriage. In their 2012 submission to the Senate, the ACL argued that same-sex marriage need not be legalised because the Parliament had already legislated against discrimination on the basis of sexuality.

As they wrote, *"Non-discrimination against same-sex couples is exactly what Federal Parliament achieved in 2008 when over 80 pieces of legislation were amended by a bipartisan majority. Homosexual couples now enjoy effective equality with married couples in every way short of marriage."*

This is the crux of the matter.

If all Australians have the same legal rights, and same-sex couples receive the same legal rights as heterosexual couples, why oppose marriage? The answer is simple: marriage has the place of honour at the heart of society.

To share that place of honour with gays and lesbians is to accept that the lifelong commitment of two gay men or two lesbian women to each other is as meaningful as the lifelong commitment of a man and a woman to each other.

People who are saying *"Don't call it marriage"* are arguing *"Don't call them my equal"*.

This is why the concept of civil unions is opposed.

As Stephanie Bolt, the sister of Andrew Bolt said, *"Offering civil unions seems a reasonable compromise from the position of any straight person who has never had to question for a single moment others' acceptance of their relationship or their right to choose to marry the person they love. Offering civil unions sends a signal that, to me, says I am lesser."*[107]

Marriage is more than a piece of paper. It has formidable social power. In exchange for a couple's promise of lifelong love and support, the institution of marriage provides acceptance of and support for the relationship that is, with the exception of children, the most important relationship in our adult life.

Constitutional lawyer Professor George Williams argues that civil unions or a system of government registration will never have the same symbolic and social power as marriage. In his words:

> *"Nothing competes with marriage for its iconic status, the symbolism that it contains within our society. I am not sure it would be possible to set up a different way of recognising a relationship that could be seen within the eyes of the broader community as being of equivalence. Of course, that is what it is about. It is about an equality and equivalence. I think even in countries where they have had [relationship] registration schemes it has not prevented the debate moving onto a marriage debate as it has here."*[108]

Over the years, state governments and local councils in Australia have offered relationship registration schemes. To be honest, does anyone want to be registered? It sounds like something you do for a dog or a cat.

At one point, the Australian Capital Territory offered same-sex marriage, until eventually it was struck down by the High Court. While I understand the good intentions behind it, it was not the real deal. It did not have the full authority of the Commonwealth of Australia. As such, the relationships would not necessarily be recognised in other parts of the country.

Anyone can buy a knighthood from the Hutt River Province but it's not the real deal. State, territory and local relationship schemes are not the real deal. They try to fill a gap because of the failure of the

Commonwealth, but they are a reflection of an incomplete citizenship.

They also reflect an implied acceptance of the argument that gays and lesbians should accept civil unions or registrations because their relationships are *'equal but different'*. The proponents of such a view argue that same-sex relationships are deserving of recognition but not deserving enough to be called a marriage. In other words, they are counterfeits or photocopies of an original work. Their relationships might seem like love, but they are not love. This is not progress, and it is why this 'compromise' is rightly ignored.

Equal means equal; it doesn't mean different.

I believe the reason why equal means equal is because we are also referring to the equality of promises. If two people take vows before others to love, honour and care for each other, to forsake all others, to love them through good times and bad, until the end of their days, then that should be called a marriage, because that is exactly what it is.

10. ARGUMENT: Australia is not ready for same-sex marriage – we should wait

There was a time when this argument might have been valid. Sometimes, the best test of change is time. Time sifts arguments. Fads come and go, but changes that suit the age grow with time.

Australia has tested the arguments for same-sex marriage. Our country has been debating this issue around kitchen tables, at BBQs, in office tea rooms and on talk shows and social media for 15 years. During that time, dozens of other nations have walked a similar path. Our friends with the most similar values, the United States, New Zealand, Canada and the United Kingdom, have all recognised same-sex marriage. They have not witnessed any unforeseen consequences, nor have there been any moves to turn back.

Australians have been debating same sex marriage since the turn of the century, and we have witnessed an evolution in our thinking. In 2004, Newspoll found that 38 per cent of Australians supported same-sex marriage and 44 per cent opposed it. By 2015, Newspoll was reporting that 58 per cent supported change and 34 per cent were opposed.[109]

Newspoll's findings are reflected in other polls, including a poll taken by the Liberal Party's pollster Crosby Textor, who found that support for same-sex marriage is as high as 72 per cent.[110]

Crosby Textor also found that a majority of people identifying as religious supported same-sex marriage, including Catholics and Anglicans. In addition, they found majority support among people over the age of 55, people with children, married people and a majority of people in all states and territories.

Let me make this observation about Crosby Textor research: it's almost always right. I have seen Crosby Textor accurately predict election results down to the exact number of seats and within a few hundred votes of the final result. When Crosby Textor says that more than 70 per cent of Australians want change, you can count on it to be true.

Their findings reflect the feedback of Australians to successive Senate inquiries into same-sex marriage. In 2004, a Senate committee into same-sex marriage received 13,000 submissions, of which 26 per cent were in favour of change. In 2009, another Senate inquiry was held and it received 27,000 submissions, of which 40 per cent were in favour. In 2012, the Senate again inquired into the issue and received 250,000 submissions, with a resounding 64 per cent in support of change.

All of this reflects a sea change in public opinion that has been occurring in our country over the last 10 years. Ten years ago, I counted myself among those who opposed change. Today, I don't. That is not unique. After all, in 2004, Howard Government legislation stipulating that marriage was between a man and a woman received the support of all within the parliament.

The changes we have witnessed in public opinion have not been driven from the top-down but from the bottom-up. Until recently, most politicians did not want to voice a view on same-sex marriage because they weren't quite sure whether support or opposition would help or hinder their own interests. So it was left to the 24 million of us to have the conversation (mostly) without them.

I don't subscribe to the view that opinion polls guide morality, or that the change in public opinion is, in and of itself, a reason for change. However, marriage is a social institution, and change can only be considered if it has the consent and the blessing of the people. The evidence suggests that it does.

The call for governments to wait is a common one for all movements for social change across history. It was one of the strongest arguments put against the civil rights movement in the United States.

Wait. Wait. Wait. Delay. Delay. Delay. It is not an argument, it is a tactic. It hopes that the campaign for change will run out of steam.

The best answer to those who call for delay was written by Dr Martin Luther King when he was imprisoned in Birmingham. While in gaol, King received a letter from local clergy calling his activities "*unwise and untimely*". Despite King's adherence to non-violence, the clergy were offended by the rancour, the debate, the disorder and the rending of the social order that King's movement had provoked.

King's response in a letter from his Birmingham cell is timeless. He answers the 'wait' argument directly:

> *"I have yet to engage in a direct action campaign that was "well timed"*

in the view of those who have not suffered unduly from the disease of segregation. For years now I have heard the word "Wait!" It rings in the ear of every Negro with piercing familiarity. This "Wait" has almost always meant "Never." We must come to see, with one of our distinguished jurists, that "justice too long delayed is justice denied."

We have waited for more than 340 years for our constitutional and God given rights. The nations of Asia and Africa are moving with jetlike speed toward gaining political independence, but we still creep at horse and buggy pace toward gaining a cup of coffee at a lunch counter.

Perhaps it is easy for those who have never felt the stinging darts of segregation to say, "Wait." But when you have seen vicious mobs lynch your mothers and fathers at will and drown your sisters and brothers at whim; when you have seen hate filled policemen curse, kick and even kill your black brothers and sisters; when you see the vast majority of your twenty million Negro brothers smothering in an airtight cage of poverty in the midst of an affluent society; when you suddenly find your tongue twisted and your speech stammering as you seek to explain to your six year old daughter why she can't go to the public amusement park that has just been advertised on television, and see tears welling up in her eyes when she is told that Funtown is closed to colored children, and see ominous clouds of inferiority beginning to form in her little mental sky, and see her beginning to distort her personality by developing an unconscious bitterness toward white people; when you have to concoct an answer for a five year old son who is asking: "Daddy, why do white people treat colored people so mean?"; when you take a cross county drive and find it necessary to sleep night after night in the uncomfortable corners of your automobile because no motel will accept you; when you are humiliated day in and day out by nagging signs reading "white" and "colored"; when your first name becomes "nigger," your middle name becomes "boy" (however old you are) and your last name becomes "John," and your wife and mother are never given the respected title "Mrs."; when you are harried by day and haunted by night by the fact that you are a Negro, living constantly at tiptoe stance, never quite knowing what to expect next, and are plagued with inner fears and

> *outer resentments; when you are forever fighting a degenerating sense of "nobodiness"—then you will understand why we find it difficult to wait."*[11]

I don't equate the case for same-sex marriage to the evils of segregation, but King's response is saying don't argue that we should wait unless you have walked a mile in another's shoes.

It is easy to say we should wait if your life is not impacted by the subtleties of prejudice: the joke and turn of phrase that makes you squirm, the golf game you weren't invited to, the dinner party invitation that excluded your partner, or the promotion that you worked for and did not receive.

Ask a gay or lesbian member of the ADF who is about to be deployed what it means to wait and not to have your relationship affirmed by the country you serve.

Ask elderly parents or grandparents what it means to wait for a wedding that they might not get to see.

Ask someone who is living with a terminal illness what it means to wait.

Wait is argued by those who have never had to wait.

Same-sex marriage is not the Rubicon. We have witnessed this extension throughout much of the Western world. This change is no longer considered radical; indeed, it is the conservative extension of marriage.

More than any other argument, this one does not stack up. The call to wait is an intellectual cop-out. It is no defence of the status quo, nor is it an indictment of change. A call to wait is not an argument, it is a cop out to avoid having to decide.

In this debate, count yourself in, count yourself out, but whatever you do, don't say *wait*.

9

THE VOTE

"Respect for ourselves guides our morals, respect for others guides our manners."
- Laurence Sterne

The institution of marriage does not belong to any government or any party, nor is it the charge of any religion or movement; marriage is owned by the people.

Long before the Church claimed it as a sacrament and government claimed it as an ordinance, it was families and friends witnessing a promise of lifelong comfort and support that made a marriage.

A government may formalise marriage, and a church may bless a marriage, but it is the people who turn strangers into kin, and who affirm a marriage through their joy and celebration.

It is right that the people, through the parliament or the ballot box, affirm the right of same-sex couples to marry and in so doing, further strengthen the institution of marriage.

In 2003, a number of Canadian provinces began to allow same-sex marriages. However, there was no residency requirement for these marriages, so many Australian couples travelled to Canada to wed. However, their marriages were not recognised in Australia, and two couples subsequently applied to the Federal Court for recognition.

Fearing that the court would rule on same-sex marriage, the Howard Government amended the Marriage Act so that marriage was defined as a *"voluntarily entered-into union of a man and a woman to exclusion of all others".*

I am sanguine about the Howard Government's actions at that time. In 2004, there had been limited community debate on same-sex marriage, and community support for change stood at a little over 30 per cent. The consent and support of the people had been neither sought nor gained. It can be fairly argued that the matters before the Federal Court were about bypassing the consent of the people. Allowing same-sex marriage is a decision of magnitude, and both sides of politics were within their rights to argue that it is the role of the elected government, rather than the courts, to decide on a matter of such significance. Of course, we will never know what the inclination of the Federal Court was. It could easily have been a decision to support the status quo.

I am a traditionalist in my belief in the supremacy of the Parliament. The late US Supreme Court Justice Antonin Scalia argued that, *"it is the premise of our system that those judgments are to be made by the people, and not opposed by a governing caste that knows best."*[12] More recently, when the US Supreme Court legalised same-sex marriage, Justice Scalia wrote in dissent *"Until the courts put a stop to it, public debate over same-sex marriage displayed American democracy at its best. Individuals on both sides of the issue passionately, but respectfully, attempted to persuade their fellow citizens to accept their views."*[13]

While Australians who support same-sex marriage might disagree with Justice Scalia's judgments, his essential point was that in a democracy, the big decisions about how a society should operate are made by the people, either at the ballot box, or through their elected representatives, anything else lacks legitimacy – and I agree.

Australia has taken a long and hard road towards legalising same-sex marriage. Over the past decade, support has doubled from about one in three people in favour of change to about two in three people in favour of change. According to most polls, same-sex marriage is supported by a majority of people in every demographic, as well as a majority of people in every state.

No matter which path lies ahead – a parliamentary vote, or a national plebiscite – the result will be legitimate, and a true reflection of the will of the people. A 'yes' vote in the parliament or in a plebiscite, will reflect the consent, the blessing and the support of the Australian people for same-sex marriage.

The politics of 2010-2016

As this book goes to print, we do not know what the election result will be. A re-elected Coalition Government has promised a national plebiscite by the end of 2016 and Labor has promised a parliamentary vote within 100 days of taking office. Either way, a vote is likely to be held in late 2016. But then again, when was the last time Australian politics panned out as we expected?

Since 2010, both parties have shifted their position on same-sex marriage. In the 2004, 2007 and 2010 elections, both the Coalition and Labor had policies affirming that marriage was "between a man and a woman". Momentum has since built for both sides to reconsider their position.

In 2012, Labor's National Conference affirmed its support for same-sex marriage but left the door open for a conscience vote. At the same time, Tony Abbott argued that the Coalition's position was a policy position taken to the previous election and could not be broken. The Coalition would keep its promise to voters and would vote against any bill supporting same-sex marriage. However, he left the door open for change following the 2013 election by saying, "*Our position, my position, going into the next election, is that what our policy will be is a matter for the post-election party room.*"[114] This was a significant shift in the Coalition's position.

When the matter went before the parliament in 2012, it was defeated by 98 votes to 42 with Prime Minister Julia Gillard, Deputy Prime Minister Wayne Swan and Opposition Leader Tony Abbott all voting against the bill. While opponents of same-sex marriage can point to a 56 vote margin in the 2012 vote, that margin largely reflected the fact that the Coalition voted as a bloc, which will not happen again.

In 2013, reinstalled Prime Minister Kevin Rudd committed Labor to overturning the ban on same-sex marriage. Mr Rudd argued that his change in view was the result of *"years of reflection in good Christian conscience"*.[115] Following the 2013 election, Julia Gillard, retired from elected office, announced at the Michael Kirby Lecture that she had changed her position on same-sex marriage. Other senior Labor figures such as Wayne Swan and Chris Bowen changed their position as well. Bill Shorten did not have to change his position, as he was one of the 42 MPs who had voted for same-sex marriage in 2012.

In the 2013 election, the Coalition under Tony Abbott won one of the largest electoral mandates in Australian history. With the promise of a party room decision during the term, momentum continued to build for a parliamentary vote on same-sex marriage in 2013 and 2014. During this time, Liberal members and senators who were in favour of same-sex marriage started to lend their support to the cause. Warren Entsch led the charge which was bolstered by a considered contribution to the debate from the Coalition's first openly gay parliamentarian, Senator Dean Smith. Even a Nationals MP, Darren Chester, signed on.

The Labor Party also cemented its position. Labor confirmed that its members could continue to vote according to their conscience for the time being, but that from 2019 a conscience vote would no longer be allowed, and all Labor members and senators would have to vote in favour of same-sex marriage. Just as I lamented the lack of a conscience vote on the conservative side, I was disappointed by the decision of the Labor Party to deny its own members a conscience vote. Our parliament needs people from all backgrounds, and when we prevent people from voting in line with their consciences on matters as deeply personal as this, we shut down the free expression of our elected representatives. Still, I cannot complain too much as Liberal Party discipline on this issue has been ironclad.

It was during 2015 that support for same-sex marriage became open in parts of the Liberal Party. However, this was also the year when politics intervened. In February 2015, Tony Abbott faced his *'near death'* experience surviving a party room ballot for a spill by 61 votes to 39. Mostly, the ballot was a reflection of the ideological divide in the Liberal Party, with 'small l' liberals (by and large) voting against the Prime Minister and conservatives sticking with him. The Prime Minister owed his survival to his conservative colleagues.

I had been of the view in the years preceding the February spill motion that Tony Abbott was setting the scene for a conscience vote on same-sex marriage and that even after the attempted spill, he was still toying with the idea. The Prime Minister's remarks in May 2015 hinted at that when he said, *"This is an important issue. It is not the only important issue facing our country right now, but it is an important issue. It is an issue upon which there are sharply divided views inside this parliament, inside our respective political parties and, indeed, as is well known, even inside my own family. It is important that all views be treated with respect, because this is one of those subjects upon which decent people can disagree. Now, I cannot foresee the future. I do not know how our society will develop. I do not know how this parliament will proceed in the months and years ahead. I do just make this one point, though. If our parliament were to make a big decision on a matter such as this, it ought to be owned by the parliament and not by any particular party."*[116]

It could only be owned by the Parliament if there was a free vote in the Parliament. The conservatives did not want a conscience vote and they sent the Prime Minister a clear message – a conscience vote was a line in the sand that he must not cross. By August, the matter went to the Joint Party Room, which by a two-to-one margin agreed to a plebiscite. The plebiscite was the mechanism for resolving the differences within the Coalition and for creating an outcome which, in the words of Tony Abbott, *"everyone could live with"*.

At the time, I felt uncomfortable about the decision. I believe that the Parliament is the embodiment of the people's will. The one-day party room debate felt rushed and ill-considered. It seemed like a buck-pass until after the next election, rather than a genuine attempt to reflect the people's will.

I don't believe the opponents of same-sex marriage needed to take such action. The Prime Minister's Office kept a detailed list of the positions of all members and senators. If a conscience vote has been taken in mid-2015, it would have been passed in the Senate but would have been defeated in the House of Representatives. Mostly, the numbers put the vote in the House at about 85 to 65 – and that was including the bulk of the 'undeclared' votes in the 'yes' column. However, the tide was going one way, and it was possible for another 5 to 7 votes to move into the 'yes' column. Even so, that would still have resulted in defeat by a 6 to 10 vote margin. There were no ifs, no buts, no maybes; the bill was going to be defeated.

The opponents of same-sex marriage feared a narrow defeat because it would mean that it would only be a matter of time before a future parliament voted for change. The supporters of same-sex marriage wanted a parliamentary vote on same-sex marriage because it appeared to be the easiest pathway towards victory.

On balance, I support the right of the Parliament to decide. I am genuinely torn by about the idea of a plebiscite. There is a strong case for the Parliament to decide, but I appreciate that after a 15 year debate, it's time for the people to have their say. In this chapter, I will put the arguments for both processes. Whatever happens, there will be a decision within the next 12 months on this issue – either in the Parliament or at the ballot box – and the issue could be won or lost in both scenarios.

A parliamentary vote

As a conservative, I believe in the Parliament as the embodiment of the will of the people. As Burke put it, *"Parliament is a deliberate assembly of one nation, with one interest, that of the whole; where, not local purpose, not local prejudices ought to guide but the general good, resulting from the general reason of the whole"*.[117]

Parliamentary democracy stands above every other system of government as one that safeguards liberty from tyranny. As Churchill said of the House of Commons, *"There is no situation to which it cannot address itself with vigour and ingenuity."*[118] The Parliament should always be the citadel of liberty and the guardian of our rights and responsibilities. Yet the Government has argued that this issue is too hard for the Parliament.

The Parliament has the constitutional authority to act on this matter. In 2012, following an attempt by the ACT Government to permit same-sex marriage, the High Court ruled that the Commonwealth Parliament has the constitutional authority to legislate on marriage.

The Parliament is not acting on this, just as it does not act on many matters, because of political cowardice. Many parliamentarians believe it is better to enjoy the privileges of office than to fulfil their responsibilities; namely to exercise their best judgment on difficult issues, regardless of the political cost.

If the Parliament decides to hold a plebiscite, the decision will be made by the Australian people and the Parliament will not subsequently be able to override it. The idea that the people can vote 'yes' and then parliamentarians can veto this decision by voting 'no' is unadulterated nonsense.

In putting the case against a plebiscite, many have focused on its projected $165 million cost. There is no question that this is a dead weight cost for our democracy. However, it is not an extraordinary cost. With 15 million people expected to vote, this equates to a cost of $11 per voter.

In putting the case for same-sex marriage, I have avoided the superficial arguments about 'wedding booms' and dodgy estimates from accounting firms that a plebiscite will cost $500 million, because this debate is not about money. It's about principle, it's about our citizenship and it's about honouring the lifelong devotion of two people to each other, and the value of those things is incalculable.

Marriage is a social institution that is governed by law. The Parliament has amended the Marriage Act 20 times in the past 55 years and it can do so again.

A plebiscite

If same-sex marriage is to go to a plebiscite, those who seek change must work for an overwhelming 'yes' vote. A 'yes' vote of 50.1 per cent will change the law, but a vote of 60 per cent or higher will change Australia.

An overwhelming vote will change the narrative of our country, just as the 90 per cent 'yes' vote in the 1967 Referendum recognising Aboriginal people changed us. A definitive 'yes' vote will affirm that Australians believe in the full citizenship of all citizens, free of alienation and discrimination.

A successful 'yes' vote will communicate to our country and to the world that we are not afraid of each other. It will affirm the unity we have in our diversity and the strength that can be found in our differences. Above all, it will demonstrate that we are a country that embraces all its citizens.

But that does not mean that the plebiscite won't be contested. Votes are always a choice between two opposing messages, and every vote involves a testing of arguments.

Many who are opposed to the plebiscite have argued that the campaign will be divisive. This is true, but every campaign is. People involved in politics don't fear campaigns because our country always regroups, even after the most divisive campaigns. We campaign because we want change and we believe we can make our country better. That is what democracy is about, but that does not mean it isn't testing. It is.

In early 2016, Australia's Human Rights Commissioner, Tim Wilson resigned his office to seek Liberal Party pre-selection for the seat of Goldstein. It was a bruising pre-selection contest and 48 hours before the ballot, the 300 delegates and many media outlets received an anonymous letter warning that Tim, who is gay, was *"a threat to families"*. It was an old-fashioned smear that Tim half-expected, but it still stung.

Shortly after reading the story online, I sent Tim an SMS saying, *"Hope you are not disheartened"*.

Tim's reply was *"Not disheartened. Emboldened. People keep asking if "I'm ok". The honest answer is a mix. This probably comes as a shock to some.*

But it's what I've had to live most of my adult life. Part of what drives me is my determination that I'm part of the last generation that has to put up with this shit."

There will be difficult days in a plebiscite. Hurtful things will be said. However, we should not underestimate the decency and fair-minded character of the Australian people. The pre-selectors answered the smear at the ballot box, and we can do the same.

When there are unfair attacks, they will sit on our national stage like a rotting carcass. There will be no need for howling, no need for outrage, no need for calls to apologise, because justice will be delivered at the ballot box.

It should also be remembered that some of the best minds from the Liberal Party, the Nationals, the Labor Party and the Greens will be working together for change. A compelling, positive message will undergird a very strong grassroots campaign.

Still, we can expect some difficult days. When they come, let them embolden good people to stay the course and redouble their efforts to be the last generation that has to put up with this nonsense.

Changing tactics for a plebiscite

Support for same-sex marriage has been above 60 per cent for at least two years.

However, there are no certainties in politics and the decision of voters is determined by a myriad of factors.

The decision of voters is usually based on a mix of rationality, emotion and instinct. A majority of voters rationally accept the case for same-sex marriage, but if they detect hubris, arrogance or a tendency to bully their opponents, that majority could easily become soft.

My considered view is that there are six areas where the supporters of same-sex marriage must change their strategy in order to achieve an overwhelming win in a national plebiscite.

1. Welcome all conversations

The opponents of same-sex marriage know they will lose a plebiscite that is about the merits of legalising same-sex marriage, but they can win a plebiscite if they make the public debate about something else.

The underlying message that the opponents of same-sex marriage will run is the issue of freedom. This is ironic, given they are opposing extending the freedom to marry to gay and lesbian people.

Already, supporters of same-sex marriage have made missteps. Some have embraced the American political tactic of identifying ways of shutting down your opponents' message.

In 2015, the Marriage Alliance group, which opposes same-sex marriage produced a TV ad putting its case. The ad was like watching paint dry. Foxtel and Channel 9 ran the ad, but following complaints on Twitter, Channel 7 and Channel 10 pulled it from the air. The radio station Nova refused to run the ad as well.

Along the way, some people lodged complaints with the Australian Communications and Media Authority (ACMA) and others signed online petitions calling for the ad to be stopped, but the law prevailed, with ACMA finding that the ad did not breach media standards.

Banning ads sets a dangerous precedent. It could mean that in future elections, party officials will lobby broadcasters about the ads of their opponents. It could see food retailers encouraging TV companies to remove ads about the treatment of animals. It could see mining magnates twist the arms of broadcasters not to run ads on climate change. Ultimately, it means that the airways, which are owned by the public, will no longer be free.

If that becomes the case, there will be a strong argument for legislative protection of free speech for our radio and TV broadcasters.

In addition, we have seen activists call on hotels to shut down meetings held by opponents of same-sex marriage and we have witnessed one major employer, PwC, demand that one of its employees, who happens to be a Christian, not participate in the campaign against same-sex marriage. PwC is proud of the many awards it has received for diversity, but it's clear that PwC only believes in diversity for some, but not for all.

Following these actions, some activists have given themselves high fives, believing they have advanced the cause. On the contrary, they are ceding the moral high ground to the opponents of same-sex marriage.

Indeed, when Telstra changed its position on same-sex marriage because of a threat by the Catholic Church to boycott it, people were right to question the appropriateness of the Church's action.

Overreach never works. We saw this again when Bendigo Bank was criticised in its local newspaper for not publicly endorsing the campaign for same-sex marriage. The 'big four' banks, along with over 800 businesses across Australia had lent their support to the campaign, but Bendigo Bank chose not to, saying, *"We feel that by taking a position as a corporate entity we are presuming the opinion of the people we work with and serve. These are very personal matters that we should and will leave to individuals to express their own views."*[19]

Did the bank say anything offensive? No. Did it discriminate against its employees? No. Did the bank refuse to give loans to same-sex couples? Not as far as we know.

It was attacked for not saying anything! The bank had thoughtfully considered the issue and decided that it was an issue for citizens, not corporations. If integrity is being true to self, then on this issue,

Bendigo Bank acted with integrity.

This debate cannot become one that is hijacked by 'well intentioned' calls for boycotts, by silencing the opposition or by shutting down people in the public domain. We have to stick to the main game of convincing people through the strength of our arguments. If this plebiscite becomes a de-facto debate about freedom and political correctness, we can easily lose it.

Our campaign is about making Australia a better place. It's about more freedom not less; more diversity, not less; more acceptance, not less – and everything we do must reflect that.

If the plebiscite turns into three months of calling for people to be fired, or for speakers to be shut down, or for ads to be banned, then the very message that we seek to propagate will be undermined. People will see it for what it is, replacing one set of prejudices with another.

During the 2010 election campaign, Tony Abbott announced his determination to "stop the boats". If I had a dollar for every time I wrote "stop the boats" during my years with him, I could retire today. Let me propose a line to be used in every interview, in every interaction in the community, in every discussion in community centres and town halls: *"We welcome all conversations."* This must be an underlying value of this campaign.

Yes, some people on the other side will say outrageous things. But these injustices should embolden us, rather than turn us into sooks who are looking for a sand-castle to kick down. We must not be dragged into the fray. We must let the unfair attacks sit in the public square as proof of why there must be change. What matters in a campaign is the vote. The express will of the Australian people in a plebiscite is a truer reflection of our country than a nasty brochure or TV ad.

The key to holding the moral high ground is letting our opponents be heard. If this debate is about the arguments, we will win. However, if it is about their freedom to be heard, it will be a close-run race.

Let's welcome all conversations, even if at times it feels uncomfortable.

2. Recognise that social media is just one tool in a grass-roots campaign

One of the misplaced assumptions of our age is that social media activity constitutes real engagement with other people.

Clicking 'like' or 'share' on a bus while heading to work is not real engagement and it's even less so if you are anonymous. It rarely involves great bravery, leadership or fortitude.

Don't get me wrong, there is value in online participation, but not as much as you might think. Mostly, we interact online with groups who share similar views to our own.

The danger in this campaign is that the supporters of same-sex marriage will like, share and post, and demand that people read articles that confirm their existing point of view, rather than engage in real campaigning or discussion.

All too often, when a different view is expressed online, a 'pile on' against the dissenting person takes place. The comments start rolling in, *"How can you believe this"*, *"I am disappointed"*, or *"What right do you have to force your views on me"*, or even *"Read this article"* which is a coded way of saying *"You are wrong."*

To win this ballot, where every citizen's vote is equal, we need advocates who will listen rather than argue. We need people to say *"Can we have a coffee?"*

Winning this debate won't happen by telling people they are wrong, or shutting them down because we don't agree with their view. It will happen by winning people over – by actually talking to them and addressing their fears.

All too often, social media has become a place to bully rather than to engage. Most days see people searching, tweeting and reporting on the views of others. Clumsy comments, silly analogies and typos quickly get a going over by self-righteous keyboard warriors. Anger and derision reaches up from below the surface. Outrage then kicks into gear, apologies are demanded, self-flagellation is expected and the 'offender' is required to be silent for a season. The tragedy is that social media activists are becoming everything they once despised.

Winning this vote doesn't just require a change in behaviour on social media. It also requires supporters of same-sex marriage to reach out into the community. Being a 'keyboard warrior' involves little effort, but speaking at a public meeting, or handing out leaflets at a shopping centre or a polling booth takes strength. It requires you to stand up for your convictions so that other people, who might not be your friends, see it.

For this campaign to be truly successful, it must reach deep into the community. It must move beyond our inner cities and reach the suburbs, the regional centres and the country towns.

It is worth recalling the lesson of the civil rights movement, whose success lay in holding the high ground and refusing to engage in the same tactics as their opponents. Dr King said *"The arc of the moral universe is long, but it bends towards justice."*

Those wanting change must demonstrate an integrity that outshines their opponents. At the shopping centres where the card tables are set up by the opposing camps, offer your opponent a cup of tea, share the biscuits, show kindness and confound their worldview with goodness. Don't raise your voice in argument, be polite and be willing to 'agree to disagree'.

We don't win people over through arguments; we win them over through actions. We own the high ground, and we should stay on the high ground.

3. Don't let the debate be hijacked

Campaigns are always about focus. Inevitably, some will use the debate to argue about tangential issues. This may feel good, but it will do nothing to advance the case for change.

If the other side raises a tangential issue, it will be because they have researched it and have found a hook to reel us in. Equally, there will be those who want to use the debate to argue about the tax deductibility of churches, the need to end discrimination in religious schools, the merits of the Safer Schools programme, or any other issue that rocks their boat.

If we take the bait, we weaken the case for change and our capacity to deliver a compelling win at the plebiscite.

4. Tell your story

It was during 2012 that Tony Abbott received a request from one of his local Liberal Party branch presidents asking for a meeting to discuss same-sex marriage. The local branch president had been in a same-sex relationship for many years, and had supported Tony Abbott for more than a decade.

The day arrived and the branch president arrived at Tony Abbott's office with his partner. He said, "*I know I can't change your mind on same-sex marriage, but I would like to tell you about my life, and our lives, and what it would mean to us if we could get married.*"

The three of them talked for an hour. They didn't argue. They simply tried to understand each other. Abbott, when he is thinking, runs his hands through his thinning hair and sometimes rubs his face, and it was clear to those in the meeting that this was a genuine interaction. It had more impact than a decade of Q&A programmes. It was real, heart-felt and authentic.

A short time later, there was another request for a meeting from a well-known activist who lived in Warringah. The time for the meeting was set, but shortly before it was due to be held, the activist let it be known publicly that he was going to confront Tony Abbott and tell him that he must vote for same-sex marriage. He had turned the proposed appointment into a stunt, and thus the drawbridge went up in response to similar requests.

People's stories are powerful. Josh Frydenberg, a conservative and supporter of Tony Abbott, was opposed to same-sex marriage but personal meetings with constituents made him reconsider. He said of one meeting with a lesbian couple that it *"ended in tears and that did have an effect on me."*[20]

Polls have shown that support for same-sex marriage is always 10 per cent to 25 per cent higher amongst people who actually know a gay or lesbian or same-sex couple. Sharing personal stories and engaging with people's genuine fears is the only way we change people's minds. There is only one way to win a plebiscite – vote by vote.

5. Welcome everyone

Senator Ricky Muir was once asked by his wife *"What would you do if your son was gay?"*[121] Muir replied. *"I'd disown him."*

He realised as soon as he said it that it *"was a bad thing to say"* and it led one of the quietest voices in the Senate to reflect on what he really thought about gay and lesbian people. Muir was unable to reconcile his prejudice with his perspective as a parent, and he subsequently announced that he supported same-sex marriage.

Ricky Muir is not alone. According to polls, support for same-sex marriage has doubled in a decade. People are changing their minds. However, they need the freedom to do so.

Had Ricky Muir made his comments on national television, he would have been rightly condemned. After all, who can condone a father disowning his son, especially when it is for no other reason than his sexuality. However, the public attacks would likely have boxed Muir into a corner from where he would not have had the freedom to reconsider his view.

One of the emotional challenges for the long-term supporters of same-sex marriage is to welcome everyone onto the bandwagon – including latecomers who have not put in the hard yards. I can understand why someone who has supported same-sex marriage for 10 years might be suspicious of Tony Abbott's speechwriter publicly joining the cause months before a plebiscite or a parliamentary vote.

But fighting yesterday's battles never helps us to grow stronger. Through patience and respect, we give people the space to change their minds, and we give them the freedom to reconcile the differences between their beliefs and their life experiences.

Those who know me know of the influence President George H.W. Bush has had on my life and political philosophy. Recently, the 91-year-old was asked what he thought of same-sex marriage. President Bush's answer captured the essence of his conservative temperament and the decency of his Christian faith:

> *"Personally, I still believe in traditional marriage. But people should be able to do what they want to do, without discrimination. People have a right to be happy. I guess you could say I have mellowed."*[22]

There will come a day when Tony Abbott will attend his lesbian sister's wedding. Other conservative leaders and commentators will be invited to similar family weddings as well. When those days come, we should let the joy stand. The tweets reminding everyone of things said long ago will add nothing. We should not worry about where people once were, but rather should commit ourselves to creating a movement where everyone is welcome.

6. Don't be sore winners

It was Andrew Sullivan, a conservative gay Catholic, who wrote *Virtually Normal* in 1995 and first put the conservative case for same-sex marriage. Sullivan argued, as I do, that same-sex marriage represents the triumph of conservatism rather than its decline.

More recently, following the US Supreme Court ruling allowing same-sex marriage in all 50 states, Sullivan issued a warning. Speaking at my alma mater, the Harvard Kennedy School, he implored supporters of same-sex marriage, *"Don't be sore winners."* He said there is a *"danger of clinging to the politics of oppression. The gay community needs to learn to take yes for an answer. It is in danger at the moment of overplaying its hand and being sore winners in this extraordinary moment and seeking to actively punish and penalise and ostracise people with whom we may disagree."*[123]

Reflecting on the changes that had occurred since he wrote *Virtually Normal*, Sullivan said, *"We now have majority support and I don't want the majority to behave like the majority did when we were the minority"*. Sullivan is reminding us that while the movement in support of same-sex marriage is a good thing, it should not be seen as an opportunity to lord it over those who disagree. A 'winner takes all' approach will diminish us as a people.

Justice Margaret Marshall, the Chief Justice of the Massachusetts

Supreme Court who wrote the judgment in *Goodridge vs Department of Public Health*, which legalised same-sex marriage in the state, issued a similar warning when she recently said *"We are a country being driven by polarisation"*.

Chief Justice Marshall's point is that we all have a responsibility, no matter what side of the debate we are on, to work through our differences. Australians must resist the *Americanisation* of our politics. This Americanisation says that we must question the integrity of those who oppose us. As the editor of *Spiked*, Brendan O'Neill put it. *"If you oppose gay marriage, you're a homophobe. If you dislike Israel, you're an anti-Semite. If you want out of Brussels, you're xenophobic. All politics is now just slander."*[124]

When we argue that our opponents lack integrity for holding a different view, that they are the cause of all our ills, and that they should be silenced, we strip them of their personhood. At that point, we see an acceleration of a vicious cycle where arguments are dismissed as motives and discourse is silenced. Ask any long-term couple; the most dangerous time in a relationship is not when voices are raised, but when there is silence. We are all the poorer when debate is silenced.

Our work is to keep this debate above the decay of modern political discourse. It is to lift the debate above the fray of Twitter, of instant responses, of boycotts of businesses that disagree and to make it as easy as possible for people to cross over.

This is the chance to welcome new friends, to celebrate our modern Australia and to make the vote – be it a parliamentary vote or a plebiscite – a celebration of our national unity.

10

THE HOPE

I was meeting with friends before a Liberal Party dinner marking the 20th anniversary of the election of the last Liberal Government in NSW.

It was a Friday night, and we met in a pub just around the corner from where the dinner was to be held. The pub was loud and boisterous, but it was a chance to talk freely with a few friends.

While I had cut my teeth as a young political staffer in the Greiner Government, there were other reasons why I wanted to be at the dinner. The dinner was bringing together the good and the great of the Liberal Party, and as I was on the shortlist to become the next state director, it was smart to be there.

During the pre-dinner drinks with my friends, we reviewed my prospects and I was given their collective lay of the land. I wasn't convinced about my prospects, and said, "*What about this guy Simon Berger? He's Brendan Nelson's senior adviser* (who was then Opposition Leader). *If the leader wants him he'll get him, that's how it works.*"

"*Paul, don't worry about Berger.*"

"*Why's that?*" I asked.

"*Because he's G-A-Y gay.*"

A chill went through me.

One of my oldest mates was dissing someone because that person was gay.

"Surely that doesn't come into it," I said somewhat lamely.

"*Paul, it's poison*" and the banter continued, mostly at Berger's expense.

At dinner, I made polite conversation, but my head was spinning. I felt cheap. I couldn't believe that I had been part of such a conversation. Mostly, I couldn't believe my own silence.

The conversation about the position of state director resumed over dinner, and as I expected that the other contenders would also be present, I asked the person sitting next to me, "*So is Berger here?*"

"*Yeah, that's him over there.*"

I resolved to introduce myself and to show the man a little of the decency I hadn't afforded him earlier in the night.

"*Simon, I'm Paul Ritchie. I want to wish you luck for the director's gig. I've heard good things about you.*" It wasn't the most truthful sentence, but it seemed a nice way to start a conversation.

Before long, we were sitting and chatting as the room cleared and we discovered a mutual admiration for anything to do with the 1980s. By the end of the night, I'd made a friend, even if I still felt slightly ashamed about what had prompted it all.

As events turned out, I pulled out of the race because I had been accepted into a masters program at Harvard University, and the job went to the Party's state director from Western Australia.

On my return from Harvard, Simon and I found ourselves in competition again. We both had eyes on pre-selection for the same seat. This time, Simon answered the talk head on. The front page of the *Sydney Morning Herald* ran the headline: *Proud to be gay, the Liberal with an eye on the safest of seats.*

It was an audacious attempt to end the whispers. I knew it wasn't going to help his prospects, but by God, I admired it.

Liberal Party pre-selection contests are a strange beast. In addition to a set-piece speech and a Q&A in front of about 200 delegates and observers, the candidates have to go through a form of speed dating where they meet with 15 tables of ten people for ten minutes each. Nothing is off-limits and the pre-selectors press and prod the candidates on every conceivable issue.

On most tables, Simon was asked, "*What's your view on gay marriage?*"

No, no one was prejudiced, of course not, but the prevalence of the question indicated the fear that his candidacy generated in many delegates. It was the modern equivalent of the question that was asked regularly of women candidates a generation ago: "*So have you thought about the impact of your candidacy on your children?*"

At none of the speed dating tables or in the Q&A session in front of the assembled delegates was I asked for my view about same-sex marriage. If I was, I had already resolved to tell the truth. After all, months earlier, I had been asked by my best mate to be best man at his same-sex wedding in Tahiti.

Simon and I both crashed and burned in the pre-selection. We were beaten by a Howard Government chief-of-staff Paul Fletcher, who is a smart and decent guy, and who ran an honourable pre-selection campaign. While no one likes losing, it somehow wasn't that hard for either of us to roll up our sleeves and work on Paul's campaign.

Whatever publicity Simon generated with his *Sydney Morning Herald* story, it was nothing compared to the furore that would occur a few years later. It was September 2012, and Simon had agreed to MC a dinner hosted by the Sydney University Liberal Club. It was the night the guest speaker said that Julia Gillard's father had "*died of shame*". It was a terrible thing to say, and Simon didn't say it. However, he was there, and that was enough for the nation's keyboard warriors.

Within days, thousands of people had petitioned Simon's employer to sack him. It was all pretty ugly. In the midst of the online pitchforks that were being hurled at Simon, his dad died. It was a bruising time for him, and I wasn't alone in wondering if he could come through this with his open and warm outlook on life still intact.

He did, but it wasn't an easy path.

Eventually, Simon and I found ourselves working together on the 2013 Federal election campaign, and that continued throughout the two years of the Abbott Government. Somehow, our friendship sat easily within the environment of continual competition that it was exposed to, as well as the occasional blow-up that occurs when you work in an environment where the pressure is high, the timeframes are short and the best judgments depend more on nuance than on strong convictions.

Through it all, I admired his honesty, the ease with which he felt comfortable in his own skin and the grace with which he withstood the slings and arrows of others. I've always believed that the best friends you can have are those who make you want to be a better person and that is the case with Simon.

It was in late 2015 that we both found ourselves at the wedding of a former Coalition staffer. It was a happy occasion as the two families celebrated the character and achievements of the children they loved and welcomed the partner whom their children had chosen to marry. As the speeches were given and the toasts were drunk, you could feel that quiet, ambient joy that comes from the love of family and friends gathering together. It felt like a whisper of the same joy I'd felt on my own wedding night.

Late in the evening, the dance floor was in full swing. There were young children in miniature tuxes and gowns jumping up and down and chasing each other, there were young men and women dancing with the passion of those whose dreams are still ahead of them and there were older couples, quietly savouring the love and joy that surrounded them.

Sarah and I danced our way through more than a few '80s classics and then sat out a few. I saw Simon standing apart from the throng. I went over to him, we clinked beer bottles and chatted about the day that was.

We were both looking at the dance floor when Simon said something I didn't expect.

"*I wonder if I'll ever get married?*" he said wistfully.

"*It would be nice. It really would.*"

The raw honesty of a friend caught me off guard.

For some time I had questioned if I should write this book, and it was at that moment that I realised I had to.

Simon's hope is a universal one: to be blessed by family and friends, and to share your life, with its trials and tribulations, laughter and joy, with the one that you love.

For some, same-sex marriage is about social change, but for most gay, lesbian, bisexual, transgender and intersex Australians, it means so much more.

It's an affirmation that our country values every one of its sons and daughters, and sees in them the full hope of our citizenship.

To gay and lesbian teenagers, it says they can have relationships as rich, meaningful and enduring as those of their parents and grandparents. By offering the same roadmap for life as we offer their brothers and sisters, we affirm their lives and their hopes. When these teenagers look at their lives, we give them another reason to say, "*I'm OK.*"

Time waits for no man or woman, and no government or law. Many, like Tim Wilson, wear engagement rings as a promise to their partner and a reminder of a glorious day ahead. As Tim says, "*Ryan and I have been engaged for six years. There are thousands of couples like us.*"

Their days are no different from anyone else's. They battle traffic, pay their taxes, try to balance work and family, follow sports teams, care for sick relatives, pay off their homes and put money aside for their retirement.

Gay and lesbian couples aren't asking anyone to buy them a cake or pay for a wedding reception; they are just asking their country to affirm their lifelong relationship and treat them no better and no worse than any other Australian couple. In the words of Andrew Sullivan, "*We need nothing from you and have much to give back to you.*"

Tens of thousands of couples like Tim and Ryan live out the practicalities of a married life, but they do so without the institutional strength of marriage. They are married and unmarried at the same time, acknowledged but not affirmed, accepted but not entirely embraced.

Marriage, in the words of the columnist David Brooks, "*makes us better than we deserve to be.*" Our lives are always better when they are shared, and they are more meaningful when others are at their centre. In life's dark times, we are strengthened, and in the good times, our joys are multiplied.

Gay or straight, young or old, rich or poor, we all face doubts about our lives. Marriage calls us to look beyond our imperfections and to see our better selves – and it allows us to be loved for who we are.

Fear about same-sex marriage blinds us to its hopes. It blinds us to the potential of sons and daughters, grandsons and granddaughters, and bringing the person they love into our families. It blinds us to their joy.

In opening up our families to our gay and lesbian sons and daughters, we make our families stronger. Marriage legally opens the door to the person they love. Instead of being separate from family, they become family and in so doing, embrace it even more. In this, married same-sex couples become a reflection of the deepest of conservative values – the strengthening of the ties between the living, the dead and the as yet unborn.

This is not a forsaking of tradition; it is a tender embrace of it.

Conservatism has always been a philosophy of dignity and respect. It understands the yearnings of people for a better life. It seeks not to discard the past, but to build on it. In the words of C. S. Lewis, *"progress means not just changing, but changing for the better."*[125]

We know that marriage is not a granite institution that cannot change, for the institution renews itself as surely as the leaves of spring unfold. To let it be unchanging in changing times is to let it become brittle, isolated and incapable of serving a new generation in need of its strength and protection.

Gay, lesbian, bisexual, transgender and intersex Australians don't seek to change marriage; rather, they seek to join it and share in its bounty and strength. This is not revolutionary, but evolutionary. It recognises what has already occurred within society, and reflects the learned truth that sexuality is not character, and our differences are not threats.

We see in same-sex marriage an opportunity for more Australians to be affirmed and strengthened as they embark on their most personal journey in life. As E.J. Graf puts it, *"What the law can do is recognise the single most important relationship most human beings throughout history have had: the one in which we share our bodies and our daily lives"*.

We also see an affirmation that we are more than flesh and blood, and muscle and sinew. We are people who believe, who hope and who love – and we have come to understand the eternal truth:

> Three things will last forever – faith, hope, and love – and the greatest of these is love.

Same-sex marriage is not the rejection of conservative values; it is the deepest embrace of them. It is not the rejection of Christian values; it is the living out of them.

As the door to marriage opens, so too does the responsibility to honour and cherish the institution. As Andrew Bolt wrote following the Irish Referendum, *"The battle for same-sex marriage has been won. Now the winners must defend marriage as fiercely as we conservatives tried.*[126]*"*

A 'yes' vote in the Parliament or in a plebiscite means that the baton of responsibility to protect our most fundamental institution will be carried by all Australians, no matter their sexuality – and this is a good thing for gay, lesbian, transgender, bisexual and intersex Australians, for the children of same-sex parents, for families, for the institution of marriage, and ultimately, for our country.

Acknowledgements

At the start of Chapter 1 I wrote that this is a book that I did not expect to write. I end the book by adding, that it is a book that I thoroughly enjoyed writing.

It is also a book that is the result of the faith and confidence of others in me.

While he might not agree with this book's conclusions, I express my gratitude to Tony Abbott for the opportunities he has given me. Working as his Press Secretary in Opposition and as his Senior Adviser and Head of Communications when he was Prime Minister was a great privilege.

My admiration for Tony knows no end. He is a man of intellect, integrity and decency and I'm proud to call him a friend.

I worked in an outstanding office and pay tribute to my smart and talented workmates. In particular, I acknowledge Peta Credlin and Andrew Hirst who are two of the finest political operatives that I have worked with.

I am grateful to my communications team who I relied on every day: Sam Groves, Sam Jackson-Hope, Kieran Walton and Jason Deutsch are all outstanding individuals. I also acknowledge the dedication of the PM&C speechwriters who deserve better recognition and support than the department gives them.

Louise Ahern was generous in her comments and advice on the manuscript and I thank her for her support during my time in the PMO.

Tim Wilson, Trent Zimmerman, Rodney Croome, Helen Moreland, Simon Berger, Shaun Schmitke, Tom Snow, Clint

McGilvray and Warren Entsch have provided me with encouragement at key moments along the way. My employer Ken Morrison also deserves thanks for giving me the freedom to pursue this work.

Adam Boyton is a longtime friend who is a source of continual encouragement and advice.

Stephen Steacy and I studied together at Harvard. He read my first book while he was serving with the US military in Iraq. Steve is a trusted friend who has supported me through good and bad times.

Connor Court is Australia's leading conservative publisher and I appreciate Anthony Cappello's willingness to go out on a limb with this book.

Simon Moore at Elton Ward Creative is a graphic designer with soul and this can been seen in the cover.

Sean Doyle and the editors at Lynk provided wise advice on the manuscript.

My sisters Angela and Justine have always provided me with unstinting support. This book reminded me about the importance of family. I am glad that this book is dedicated to our parents who are the foundations of our world.

Finally, I express my thanks to my wife Sarah. I have the fortune of being married to a better person, a better parent and someone who is utterly selfless. In a way that I did not expect when I started writing this book, my thoughts returned to the steadfastness of the best person I know.

Evelyn and Amelia provide Sarah and I with immense joy and I am so proud of our two girls.

Writing a book is a solitary experience and it meant that I had to shut my study door on many evenings when I should have been with my family. This book could not have been written without their blessing and support.

BIBLIOGRAPHY

Andrews, Kevin. *Maybe 'I Do': Modern Marriage and the Pursuit of Happiness*, Connor Court Publishing, 2012.

Berg, Thomas.C. What Same-Sex-Marriage and Religious-Liberty Claims Have in Common, Volume 5, Issue 2, *NorthWestern Journal of Law and Social Policy*. 2010.

Carpenter, Dale. Traditionalist Case for Gay Marriage, *Texas Law Review* 93, 2009.

Croome, Rodney. *From This Day Forward: Marriage Equality in Australia*, Walleah Press, 2015.

De Vaus, David and Qu, Lixia (Australian Institute of Family Studies). Living Alone and Personal Wellbeing.

Eskridge, William. N. A. Jurisprudence of "Coming Out": Religion, Homosexuality, and Collisions of Liberty and Equality in American Public Law, Faculty Scholarship Series, Paper 1518, 1997.

FitzSimons, Peter. *Fromelles and Pozieres In the Trenches of Hell*. Penguin Random House Australia, 2015.

Graff, E.J. *What Is Marriage For?*, Beacon Press, 1999.

Kahn, Rabbi Yoel H. The Kedusha of Homosexual Relationships, Central Conference of American Rabbis, 1989.

Lamb, Michael. *The Role of the Father in Child Development* (4th edition), Wiley Publishing 2004.

Laycock, Douglas; Berg, Thomas; Blankenhorn, David; Failinger Maria; and McGlynn Gaffney, Edward. Writs of Certiorari to the United States Court of Appeals for the Sixth Circuit (Nos. 14-556, 14-562, 14-571 and 14-574), 2015.

Locke, John. *A Letter Concerning Toleration* (Translated by William Popple), 1689.

Mackay, Hugh. *The Art of Belonging*, Pan Macmillan Australia, 2014.

Mill, John Stuart. *On Liberty*, first published 1859.

Mill, John Stuart. *The Subjection of Women*, first published 1869.

Molho, Anthony. *Marriage Alliance in Late Medieval Florence*, Harvard University Press, 1994.

Nichols L.M and Grove-Nichols, Mary. *Marriage: Its History, Character and Results*. New York, 1854.

Puplick, Christopher, and Galbraith, Larry. *Marriage Equality for All Australians: Guaranteeing security and certainty for all*, Sydney, 2014

Rauch, Jonathan. *Gay Marriage: Why it is Good for Gays, Good for Straights, and Good for America*, Henry Holt and Company, 2004

Sampson, Robert; Laub, John and Wimer, Christopher. Does Marriage Reduce Crime? A Counterfactual Approach to Within-Individual Causal Effects, *Criminology*, Volume 44, No. 3, 2006.

Sullivan, Andrew. *The Conservative Soul: Fundamentalism, freedom, and the future of the right*, Harper Collins, 2006.

Sullivan, Andrew (editor). *Same-Sex Marriage Pro & Con Reader*, Vintage Books, 2004.

Sullivan, Andrew. *Virtually Normal*, First Vintage Books, 1996.

ENDNOTES

1 http://www.blowering.com/brunglereserve.html
2 https://www.poets.org/poetsorg/poem/do-not-go-gentle-good-night
3 Cameron, David. Speech to Conservative Party Conference. 6 October 2011.
4 Sullivan, Andrew (editor). *Same-Sex Marriage Pro & Con Reader*, Vintage Books, 2004.
5 Perrottet, Dominic. "Deconstructing Greer", *The Spectator*, 23 April 2016.
6 *The Book of Common Prayer* 1549.
7 Waite, Linda. "Why Marriage Matters", *Threshold* 57:4-8.
8 Schoonboen, C.A. "Marital Status and health: United States, 1999-2002 Advance data from vital and health statistics; No 351, National Centre for Health Statistics (2004).
9 Hamish, G. Leonard, K. and Cornelius J. "illicit Drug Use and Marital Satisfaction", *Addictive Behaviours* 33.2 (2008): 279 - 291.
10 Franks, Melissa., Pienta, Amy. and Wray, Linda. "It takes two: Marriage and Smoking Cessation in the Middle Years", *Journal of Ageing and Health*, (2002), Vol 14, No 3, 336-354.
11 Whitlock, G. Norton, R. Clark, T. Jackson, R. and MacMahon, S. "Motor vehicle driver injury and marital status: a cohort study with prospective and retrospective driver injuries", *Injury Prevention*, 2004;10:33-36.
12 Schoonboen, C.A. "Marital Status and health: United States, 1999 - 2002 Advance data from vital and health statistics; No 351, National Centre for Health Statistics (2004)
13 Zhang, Zhenmei and Hayward, Mark D. "Gender, the marital life

course, and cardiovascular disease in late midlife", *Journal of Marriage and Family* 68: 639 - 657 (2006).

14 Amato, Paul. "Marriage, cohabitation and mental health", *Family Matters* 2015, No 96.

15 Zimmerman, A.C., & Easterlin, R.A. "Happily ever after? Cohabitation, marriage, divorce and happiness in Germany". *Population and Development Review*, 32(3), 511- 528 (2006).

16 Soons, J., Liefbroer, A. and Kalminj, M. "The Long-term consequences of relationship formation for subjective well-being." *Journal of Marriage and Family*, 71(5), 1254-1270 (2009).

17 Musick, K. & Bumpass, L. "Reexamining the case for marriage: Union-formation and changes in well-being". Journal of Marriage and Family, 74(1), 1-18 (2012).

18 Australian Bureau of Statistics. Cat No. 4130.0 – Housing Occupancy and Costs, 2013-14.

19 Australian Bureau of Statistics. Cat No. 6523.0 Household Income and Wealth, Australia, 2013-14

20 Australian Bureau of Statistics. Cat No. 6523.0 Household Income and Wealth, Australia, 2013-14

21 Wallace, Jim. Launceston Examiner, "Should we legalise gay marriage?, *Examiner*, 4 September 2009.

22 Mill, John S. *On Liberty*. 1869.

23 Australian Institute of Health and Welfare, Australia's Welfare 2015.

24 Rauch, Jonathan. *Gay Marriage: Why it is Good for Gays, Good for Straights, and Good for America*, Henry Holt and Company, 2004

25 Menzies, Robert. The Forgotten People. Speech, May 22 1942.

26 Wilson, James. Q. "Against Homosexual Marriage," *Commentary 101* (March 1996): 34-39.

27 Barnes, J. C. and Beaver, K. M. (2012), Marriage and Desistance From Crime: A Consideration of Gene–Environment Correlation. *Journal of Marriage and Family*, 74: 19–33.

28 National Archives of Australia, Series, No B2455, Barcode 4171528.
29 Bean, Charles. *Official History of Australia in the War of 1914 - 1918, Volume III.* p 408.
30 Bean, Charles. The Leadership of Norman Begins. *The Link.* 1 September 1926.
31 Abbott, Tony. Speech at Lone Pine Commemoration. 25 April 2015.
32 Burke, Edmund. *Reflections on the Revolution in France.* 1790.
33 Menzies, Robert. Speech at Laying of the Foundation Stone, 25 August 1963.
34 Transcript of Interview with Dr Martin Luther King Jr. by Mike Wallace. 25 June 1958.
35 Alan Brownstein, The Right Not to Be John Garvey. *Cornell Law Review.* 767, 807. 1998.
36 Leyonhjelm, David. Hansard. 26 November 2014.
37 US Court of Appeals for the Ninth Circuit. Perry v Brown. No 10-16696. 7 February 2012
38 Broome, Rodney. *Hobart Mercury.* Talking Point: Time to lay ground rules for respectful marriage equality debate. 24 December 2015.
39 Mill, John Stuart. *The Subjection of Women.* 1869.
40 Burke, Edmund. *Reflections on the Revolution in France.* 1790.
41 Meacham, Jon. *Destiny and Power: The American Odyssey of George Herbert Walker Bush.* Random House. 2015.
42 Sullivan, Andrew. *The Conservative Soul: Fundamentalism, freedom, and the future of the right*, Harper Collins, 2006.
43 Graff, E.J. *What Is Marriage For?*, Beacon Press, 1999.
44 Blackstone, William. Commentaries on the Laws of England. 1765-1769.
45. Gallup Research. http://www.gallup.com/poll/163697/approve-marriage-blacks-whites.aspx
46 Graff, E.J. *What Is Marriage For?*, Beacon Press, 1999.
47 Croome, Rodney. *From This Day Forward: Marriage Equality in Australia,*

Walleah Press, 2015.

48 C. H. Currey, 'Bryant, Mary (1765–1794)', *Australian Dictionary of Biography*, National Centre of Biography, Australian National University. 1966.

49 Commonwealth of Australia. http://www.australia.gov.au/about-australia/australian-story/convicts-and-the-british-colonies

50 Broome, Rodney. A History of Marriage in Australia. *The Drum*. 1 July 2011

51 Department of Immigration and Border Protection. Fact sheet: Abolition of the White Australia Policy. https://www.border.gov.au/about/corporate/information/fact-sheets/08abolition

52 Calwell, Arthur. Hansard. House of Representatives. 9 February 1949, p.63-67.

53 *The Economist*. "Let them Wed". 4 January 1996.

54 *The Times*. "For Gay Marriage; Allowing same-sex couples to marry would enrich the institution and expand the sum of human happiness". 5 March 2012

55 Australian Bureau of Statistics. 3310.0 - Marriages and Divorces, Australia, 2014.

56 Australian Bureau of Statistics. Cat No. 4442.0 - Family Characteristics and Transitions, Australia, 2012-13.

57 Australian Bureau of Statistics. 3310.0 – Marriages and Divorces, Australia, 2014.

58 Vanstone, Amanda. ABC Q&A Transcript. 5 March 2012.

59 Mill, John Stuart. *On Liberty*. 1869.

60 Brooks, David. *New York Times*. The Power of Marriage, 22 November 2003.

61 Aubusson, Kate. *Sydney Morning Herald*. 'We don't have a hallmark card relationship': Peter FitzSimons speaks candidly about marriage to Lisa Wilkinson", 28 March 2016.

62 Dane, Sharon, Masser, Barbara., MacDonald, Geoff, and Duck, Julie.

Not so private lives: National findings on the relationships and well-being of same-sex attracted Australians. Version 1.1. The University of Queensland.

63 HM The Queen. Message to the Service of Remembrance. 20 September 2001.

64 Pell, Cardinal George. Submission to the Senate Legal and Constitutional Affairs Committee Inquiry into the Marriage Equality Amendment Bill 2009. 28 August 2009.

65 Australian Bureau of Statistics. Cat. 3310.0 - Marriages and Divorces, Australia, 2014.

66 House Standing Committee on Social Policy and Legal Affairs. Summary of Responses: Inquiry into the Marriage Equality Amendment Bill 2012 and the Marriage Amendment Bill 2012.

67 Massachusetts Supreme Court. *Goodridge*, 798 N.E.2d. at 965 n.29. 2003.

68 Kirby, Michael. The Worrying Decline of Secularism. interview with Patti Shih, PhD Candidate, School of Public Health and Community Medicine, University of New South Wales. November 2010.

69 Kelly, Paul. *The Australian.* The same-sex marriage debate and the right to religious belief. 11 July 2015.

70 Berg, Thomas.C. What Same-Sex-Marriage and Religious-Liberty Claims Have in Common, Volume 5, issue 2, *Northwestern Journal of Law and Social Policy.* 2010.

71 Dane, Perry. A Holy Secular Institution. *Emory Law Journal*, Vol. 58, pp. 1123-1194, 2009.

72 National Catholic Education Commission, Catholic Schools in Australia 2016.

73 Gerson, Michael. Transcript of speech. The Pope Francis Moment. September 2015.

74 Spadaro, Antonia. A Big Heart Open to God: The exclusive interview with Pope Francis. America: *The National Catholic Review.* 30 September 2013.

75 Finger, Raymond. Submission by the Salvation Army to the Standing Committee on Social Policy and Legal Affairs, 30 March 2012.

76 Submission by the Australian Catholic Bishops Conference to the Standing Committee on Social Policy and Legal Affairs, March 2012.

77 Anglican Synod of Sydney: Submission to the House of Representatives Standing Committee on Social Policy and Legal Affairs, 30 March 2012.

78 Cook, David. Malcolm in the Middle. Moderator's Comments. presybterian.org Posted 16 February 2016.

79 Sullivan, Andrew. *Virtually Normal,* First Vintage Books, 1996.

80 Eskridge, William N. Jr., "A Jurisprudence of "Coming Out": Religion, Homosexuality, and Collisions of Liberty and Equality in American Public Law". Faculty Scholarship Series. Paper 1518. 1997.

81 Vella. Matt, "Why the world weeps for Paris". *Time Magazine.* 18 November 2015.

82 Abbott, Tony., Hansard. House of Representatives. 9 February 2015.

83 Australian Bureau of Statistics. Cat no 3101.0 Australian Demographic Statistics, September 2015 and ABS Population Clock.

84 Department of Education and Training. 2015 First half year student summary tables.

85 Department of Veterans' Affairs, DVA Pensioner Summary, September 2015.

86 Australian Bureau of Statistics, Childcare Education and Care, June 2014.

87 Department of Defence, Defence White Paper 2013, pg 104, 2013.

88 Australian Bureau of Statistics, Estimates of Aboriginal and Torres Strait Islander Australians, June 2011.

89 Australian Bureau of Statistics, Australian Social Trends, April 2013.

90 Australian Bureau of Statistics, Reflecting a Nation: Stories from the 2011 Census, 2012-2013.

91 New Zealand PM John Key to vote for gay marriage. News.com.au.

30 July 2012.

92 Ackerman, Piers. When convenience and distraction unite. News.com.au. 3 August 2009.

93 Brown, Rachel. Nationals MP Andrew Broad under fire after likening same-sex relations to 'rams in a paddock'. abc.net.au, 12 February 2016.

94 Supreme Judicial Court of Massachusetts, Ruling: Goodridge v Department of Public Health, 2003.

95 Abbott, Tony. Transcript of speech at the National Apology for Forced Adoptions. 21 March 2013.

96 Australian Bureau of Statistics, Australian Social Trends, March Quarter 2012.

97 Australian Bureau of Statistics, Australian Social Trends, July 2013.

98 Abbott, Tony. Transcript of speech at the National Apology for Forced Adoptions. 21 March 2013.

99 Obama, Barack. Remarks by the President at Sandy Hook Interfaith Prayer Vigil. 16 December 2012.

100 Lamb, Michael E. (Editor). (fifth Edition). John Wiley and Sons. 2010.

101 *Ibid.*

102 Green, R. Sexual Identity of 37 children raised by homosexual or transexual parents. *American Journal of Psychiatry*, 135, 692-697. 1978.

103 Scott v Georgia. 39 Ga Rep. 321, 324. 1869.

104 The Commonwealth of Australia Constitution Act. Section 116.

105 Gallup. Gay and Lesbian Rights. http://www.gallup.com/poll/1651/gay-lesbian-rights.aspx. Accessed 1 June 2016.

106 The Bible, New International Version, Ecclesiastes, Chapter 3.

107 Bolt, Stephanie, "Bolt: I want marriage equality for all", *Crikey* 13 January, 2011

108 Williams, George. Hansard (Committee), 12 April, 2012.

109 News poll. June 2015. http://www.theaustralian.com.au/national-

affairs/newspoll/more-australians-back-change-to-allow-samesex-marriage/news-story/1f645f84cb458c9648d9e80f0d564592

110 Crosby Textor Research 2014. http://www.crosbytextor.com/news/crosby-textor-same-sex-marriage-research-2014/

111 King, Martin Jr. Letter from a Birmingham Jail. August 1963

112 Supreme Court of the United States. No. 02 - 102, John Geddes Lawrence and Tyron Garner, Petitioners v. Texas. 26 June 2003

113 Supreme Court of the United States. Obergefell et all v. Hodges, Director, Ohio Department of Health, et al. 26 June 2015.

114 Abbott, Tony. Transcript – Lateline. 19 April 2013.

115 Rudd, Kevin. Transcript Q&A. 3 September 2013.

116 Abbott, Tony. Hansard. 27 May 2015.

117 Burke, Edmund. Speech to the Electors of Bristol. 3 November 1774.

118 Churchill, Winston. *Winston S Churchill: His Complete Speeches 1897–1963*, Vol. VII, 1943-1949, edited by Robert Rhodes James.

119 Kearney, Mark. Bendigo Bank will not disclose a position on same-sex marriage. *Bendigo Advertiser*. 29 January 2016.

120 Frydenberg, Josh. Transcript ABC Radio National. 26 March 2015.

121 ABC TV, Transcript Kitchen Cabinet. 12 November 2015.

122 Meacham, Jon. *Destiny and Power: The American Odyssey of George Herbert Walker Bush*. Random House. 2015.

123 Sullivan Andrew. Panel discussion, John F Kennedy Forum, Harvard Kennedy School. 19 October 2015.

124 O'Neill, Brendan. Facebook post. 21 Marsh 2016.

125 Lewis. C.S. *Mere Christianity*. Harper Collins, 1952.

126 *Herald Sun*. "The battle for same-sex marriage is over. Now join us to defend the institution". 27 May 2015.

www.ingramcontent.com/pod-product-compliance
Lightning Source LLC
Chambersburg PA
CBHW071838230426
43671CB00012B/1992